JACK CHRISTIE
THE WHISTLER OUTDOORS GUIDE

A Brighouse Press book
published by Douglas & McIntyre
Vancouver/Toronto

To Roger and Lillian, Bob and Jacqueline

Text and maps copyright © 1992 by Jack Christie

Douglas & McIntyre
1615 Venables Street
Vancouver
British Columbia
V5L 2H1

Canadian Cataloguing in Publication Data

Christie, Jack, 1946-
    The Whistler outdoors guide

    Includes index.
    ISBN 1-55054-021-1
    1. Whistler Mountain Region (B.C.)—Description and travel
—Guide-books. 2. Whistler (B.C.)—Description—Guide-books.
3. Outdoor recreation—British Columbia—Whistler Mountain
Region—Guide-books. I. Title.
FC3845.W59C57 1992   917.11'31044   C92-091080-7
F1089.W59C57 1992

Cover photo of Joffre Lakes Provincial Park by Paul Morrison
Photos by Louise Christie unless noted otherwise
Maps by Kelly Alm
Edited by Maja Grip
Typeset by Vancouver Desktop Publishing Centre
Printed and bound in Canada

CONTENTS

ACKNOWLEDGEMENTS

Writing this book would not have been nearly as much fun without the good company of family and friends, especially that of my wife, Louise, and our sons, Athal and Arrlann.

Over the course of researching and writing *The Whistler Outdoors Guide*, I was encouraged by many people who share my love of the region. Pioneers Rose Tatlow, editor emeritus of the *Squamish Times*, and Florence Petersen, founder of the Whistler Museum, gave generously of their time. Nora Gamboli shared memories of her mother, Joan Matthews. Perry Beckham of the Squamish Rockclimbers Association, Janet Mason, research toponymist with the Ministry of Crown Lands, and the staff at B.C. Parks (Garibaldi District) in Brackendale, at the B.C. Forest Service (Squamish District), and at the Squamish and Howe Sound Chamber of Commerce all made helpful contributions.

Cathy Dixon of Whistler Mountain and Shelley L'Estrange of Blackcomb have supported my writing for many seasons. Thanks go to Richard Benfield and the staff of the Whistler Resort Association, Jan Jensen at the Resort Municipality of Whistler, the staff of the *Whistler Question*, Richard and Leanna Rathkelly, Jackie and Jurgen Rauh, Irene Wolf, and Paul Martin.

In Pemberton, Molly Ronayne answered many questions; Charlie Hou supplied valuable information on the Gold Rush Trail.

Superb photographic assistance came from Bob Abbott and the staff at Action Reprographics, Charles Campbell of the *Georgia Straight*, Randy Stoltmann, Derrick Thompson, and Kirk Tougas.

Kelly Alm mastered the maps; Maja Grip provided editorial wisdom; Elizabeth Wilson and Terri Wershler of Brighouse Press were guiding lights. Thanks to Deborah Cochran and friends at Isadora's; Dan McLeod, Naomi Pauls and the rest of the staff of the *Georgia Straight*; Anne Penman and the staff of CBC Radio's Early Edition.

The works of Frances Decker, Margaret Fougberg and Mary Ronayne at Pioneer Pemberton Women Publishing, Mark Bostwick, Mary and David Macaree, Paul Kroeger, Anne McMahon, Maggie Paquet, Betty Pratt-Johnson, Randy Stoltmann, William Mathews, Wayne Suttles, and Richard Wright have all been helpful resources.

And finally, thanks to Featherstone & Co., who kept us in fine spirits.

LIST OF MAPS

LEGEND

ⅲⅲⅲ	Dike/dam
ᜄ	Marsh
ⓥ	Viewpoint
ⓟ	Parking
⚏	Picnic site
⚘	Campground with picnic facilities
▧	Glacier
⌃	Mountain peak
ⓘ	Information
——	Road
----	Trail
——	Railroad
•—•	Park boundary
⑨⑨	Highway
•–•	Gate
★	Point of interest
╱	Aerial tram

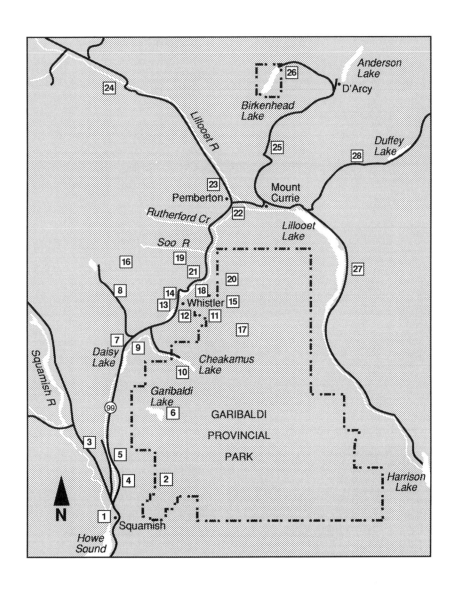

SQUAMISH |

SQUAMISH: GATEWAY
TO RECREATION

Squamish is the gateway to a recreation corridor that stretches 100 mi. (160 km) north from the mouth of Howe Sound, running through the Cheakamus Canyon to the Whistler Valley and beyond to Pemberton and the Harrison headwaters. In 1792, when Captain George Vancouver of the English fleet anchored in Howe Sound, there were 16 or more Squamish Indian villages located along the Squamish River, within 25 mi. (40 km) of its mouth. Most of these villages maintained summer camps on Howe Sound and Burrard Inlet. Two hundred years later the flow of traffic in summer is in the opposite direction, as city dwellers from Vancouver head for campsites in the Squamish region and points north. It's not unusual for our family to journey with a canoe or skis and snowboards on the roof, two mountain bikes hanging from the rack in back, and the inside of the car crammed with tennis rackets, hiking or snow boots, fishing rods, binoculars and other equipment needed for a visit to the valleys around Squamish.

Today's traffic makes its way carefully up the Squamish Highway as it hugs the hillside above Howe Sound, a deep trench carved by a retreating glacier. Many of the peaks surrounding Squamish hold the remnants of the most recent ice age. These white expanses can be seen from Vancouver, shimmering in the distance.

Because of the ocean's moderating influence, Squamish has a milder climate than the Whistler and Pemberton regions. You can cycle on bare trails or fish in open water for much of the winter here, while less than an hour's drive north everything is covered with a deep, crisp layer of snow and ice. The Squamish Indians went barefoot year-round unless they journeyed north along the Pemberton Trail in winter, in which case they wore moccasins, sometimes travelling with the help of snowshoes. The Pemberton Trail was an active trading route, part of a vast network linking the coast with villages in the interior. Travellers along the trail often brought news of sudden changes that had occurred in the course of creeks and rivers such as the Mamquam and the Squamish, the

Cheakamus and the Cheekye. Still young in geological terms, these rivers can easily be rerouted by strong floods. Gravel, silt, and fallen trees washed down by heavy rains form bars that dam the water's flow, creating new channels.

Like most cultures, the Squamish have a legend about a great flood that once covered the earth. Only one member of the Squamish tribe survived the catastrophe. Heeding a warning given to him in a vision, he took refuge on the side of Mount Garibaldi (Mount Chuckigh in the Coast Salish language spoken by the Squamish people) before the waters rose. After the flood, a great eagle brought him a salmon as a sign that life was returning to the valley below. When he descended to find his village covered with silt, he met a woman from another tribe who had also been spared. Together they took the eagle as their chief totem, a symbol revered by succeeding generations of Squamish clans.

Early Hudson's Bay explorers who walked the Pemberton Trail in 1857 were the first Europeans to see the havoc wreaked by the great landslide that had occurred two years earlier at Daisy Lake. The rumble felt then in nearby villages must have reinforced the Squamish taboo against exploring too high in the mountains for fear of incurring the wrath of the mighty Thunderbird.

As you journey through the Squamish region, keep these myths and traditions in mind. They have been formed by centuries of experience. Be prepared to meet adversity as you travel. Adversity builds character, character builds faith, and with faith you'll find your way as you adventure along these roads and trails.

1 | SQUAMISH AREA

When the first European settlers arrived in the Squamish area they farmed the open fields north of the Mamquam River. What is now downtown Squamish was used originally as pasture for beef cattle destined for market in the fledgling community of Vancouver. In 1902, the first hotel was built at a dock beside the hayfields that had supplanted the pasture. At the same time, logging in nearby Diamond Head and Alice Lake began in earnest. It quickly became the town's main industry, drawing settlers in far greater numbers than farming ever had.

The name of the town was changed in 1912 to Newport; some hoped that an anglicized name would make the town more attractive to settlers, but the change was not popular with longtime residents of the valley. When the Pacific Great Eastern Railroad established its base of operations in Squamish in 1915, the company held a contest for children throughout the province to choose a new name. A local lad won the $500 prize with his suggestion that the original name was still the best. Squamish remained the southern terminus of the railroad until a link to North Vancouver was completed in 1956. The isolation imposed on the town by the surrounding barrier of water and mountains ended two years later when the Squamish Highway was opened to the south.

For almost a century Squamish has found a warm place in the hearts of day trippers from the Lower Mainland. They have come on excursions aboard boats of the Union Steamship Line and by railcars pulled by the Royal Hudson steam engine. When residents hear the distinctive whistle of the steam engine pulling into Squamish, they automatically check their watches to see if the train's on time. Many visitors still journey this way in summer. (Call 984-5246 if you'd like to arrange to take a boat one way and return by rail to Vancouver.)

The Royal Hudson's passengers disembark at a downtown park

designed with day trippers in mind. A sheltered wooden bandstand, built for the town's centennial celebrations in 1988, stands beside the open picnic area. Next to it is the Chamber of Commerce information office on Second Avenue, a good place to find out more about events in Squamish (phone 892-9244).

In the past decade, with advances in the fields of sailboarding and rock climbing, Squamish has quietly become a world-class recreational destination in its own right, endowed with two natural drawing cards for practitioners of these sports: a strong wind that blows on Howe Sound with absolute regularity, and one of the largest outcrops of granite in the world.

SHANNON FALLS   The viewpoint of Squamish at the town's lower limits, a mile (1.6 km) south of Shannon Falls on Highway 99, marks the approach to a remarkable series of geographical formations. There's a plaque here honouring the memory of the great 19th-century Italian leader Giuseppe Garibaldi, for whom distant Mount Garibaldi is named. Fittingly, it is mounted on a large piece of granite quarried from nearby Stawamus Chief Mountain. At the same time that the granite features of the Chief catch your eye, B.C.'s third-highest waterfall presents itself for admiration.

Shannon Falls, the Chief's companion, is linked to it by a mile-long (1.6-km) trail. The white veil of water drops 1105 ft. (335 m) from a ridge above Highway 99 to a creekbed below that empties into nearby Howe Sound. Sixty years ago the falls drove a wooden waterwheel to provide energy to a nearby sawmill. A replica of the large wheel is mounted beside the creek; in a clearing not far away an impressive collection of old logging equipment lines the trail.

Shannon Falls is a popular place during summer months, and the parking lot is usually full by noon on weekends from May through September. There are two large picnic areas suited to families and

---

A LINGUISTIC PUZZLE

While there have been attempts to translate "Squamish" as an Indian expression meaning "mother of the wind," there is no linguistic root for the name. The original European explorers rarely recorded names of the native people they encountered; according to noted northwest coast anthropologist and linguist Dr. Wayne Suttles, none can be identified with names used later. The name appeared in a 1907 study as "Squawmish," referring to the Indians who still inhabit two dozen settlements along the Squamish River.

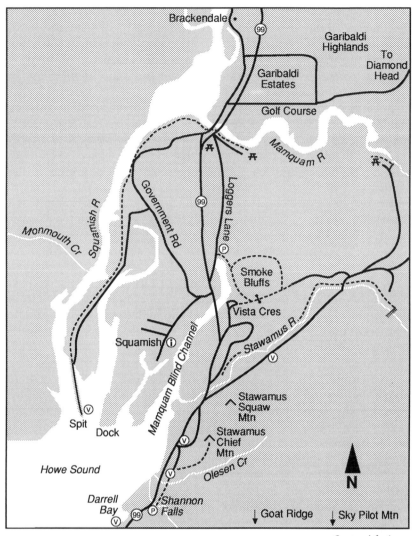

Squamish Area

groups who like room to stretch out and play while barbecuing. In the corner of one of these grassy sections is a loggers' sport area: two large tree cross-sections, painted with bull's-eyes, stand ready for axe-tossing practice. Beside them a skinned pole is propped at an angle, perfect for testing your balancing skills. A old black steam donkey engine, set up on two new wooden skids, stands in the foreground. Directly to the east the falls maintain a constant roar while the Chief's south face looms on high; many visitors take advantage of this backdrop for photographs.

It only takes a minute to walk up to the falls from the parking lot. A

Italian revolutionary Giuseppe Garibaldi's reputation was as prominent in the 1860s as the peak named in his honour.

well-built system of wooden staircases and bridges leads to a viewing platform near the base of the falls. There are some impressive trees here; several of the older ones toppled during a violent windstorm in the winter of 1990/91. Just below the platform is a rough trail that leads higher for those who like to taste the spray carried on the breeze created by the tumbling water.

The original inhabitants of Squamish have a myth about the creation of the falls. They tell of a large sea serpent called Say'noth'kai who once inhabited Howe Sound. His slithering expeditions on this mountainside gradually wore the spillway for the waters of Shannon Creek. Indeed, the wet rock face, worn smooth by the falls, does have the appearance of snakeskin.

The serpent of Shannon Falls.

Shannon Falls was established as a park in 1984. Originally it was only a small piece of land; a much larger section was acquired in 1990 to protect the site from logging. The grounds have seen many improvements as the number of visitors continues to increase.

Across Highway 99 from the park is Klahanie Lodge, a good place for refreshment. There are showers here, as well as many scenic campsites and a mountaineering shop (in case you forgot to bring your ropes). They take camping reservations at 892-3435.

STAWAMUS CHIEF There are several approaches to the base of this enormous outcrop of granite. One trail starts from Shannon Falls north of the loggers' sport area. Leave your car in the lot and look for the orange and red markers affixed to a large cedar tree by the Federation of B.C. Mountain Clubs, which point the way. Travel time to the Chief is 15 minutes on this well-maintained trail.

The first half of the trail is over level ground through an alder forest. Once it reaches the base of the mountain it begins to climb beside the smooth granite rock face, which is covered in places by green lichen. You may have to clamber over the occasional blow-down blocking the trail just before the small bridge over Olesen Creek, which gurgles down through a cleft in the mountainside. The trail to the top of Stawamus Chief Mountain begins across the creek.

The other approach allows you to drive to the base of the Chief via the designated turnoff and interpretive viewing area on Highway 99 just north of Shannon Falls. Take the dirt road leading up the embankment in the middle of the viewpoint (it's not as badly eroded as the others). It links up with a section of the old highway that runs north and south as it hugs the base of the Chief.

(If you are only interested in a quick look at the Chief, turn left on this old road. Beginning 100 yds. (30 m) along on the right, several trails lead to the base of First Peak. The southernmost trail goes to an overhang called Psyche Ledge where climbers make their mental preparations in advance of an ascent. Nearby, Squamish carver Jack Peterson has chiselled the features of a small climber on the granite wall, honouring the first full ascent of the mountain in 1962. If you continue farther, the old road soon leads back to Highway 99 next to the Stawamus River. There's quite a rock slide on the hillside above the river. A rough trail leads up to the foot of the Chief through boulders enscribed large with the names and dates of grad classes and visitors like "Maui Boy." When you stand next to the Chief here, you look up and up at a wall of smooth granite. It's awe-inspiring. You can see why this monolith has become internationally famous with climbers and graced more than its share of magazine covers. Some climbers like to overnight on the face. Bright patches of colour indicate their presence.)

To reach the trailhead to the top of the Chief, turn right onto the old road above the viewpoint, continuing on for 1 mi. (1.6 km) to its end. Along the way are many unofficial campsites for overnight visitors. More spaces are cleared each year as the licence plates come from farther away. This is a pleasant, sheltered location, with room at the end of the road for a dozen cars to park. Hiking from here to the top of the Chief will take you an hour or longer. Many families with young children visit the Chief—this is a great trail on which to let kids burn off energy. (While

9

Driving south towards Stawamus Chief, with Goat Ridge in the background.

this trail is the most popular with hikers, it is only one of the hundreds of possible routes on the Chief.)

Climb over the large boulder at the base of the trail, then begin your ascent on the beautifully groomed steps and steep staircase built by the

Federation of B.C. Mountain Clubs in 1985. The handrails are smooth and well oiled from constant use by visitors.

The bridge to the Shannon Falls trail soon appears over Olesen Creek. A little bench is provided to enjoy the good views from here out over Howe Sound. You can see the ripples where the outflow of the Squamish River meets the tidal action in Howe Sound. Several distinct shades of green delineate the zones of dissolution as fresh and salt water blend. It's also a good place to assess how much higher you want to climb. This is a steep trail, and it helps if you are psyched up to do it.

Depending on your hiking companion and how much time you have, you can pick which of the Chief's three peaks is suited to you. It's not practical to take dogs on the trail to Second and Third peaks because of a number of obstacles, including a narrow log bridge.

The three peaks share a common approach, the wood and stone stairs leading upwards beside Olesen Creek. Potholes in the creek are filled with clear water, a boon to weary hikers on descent. Keep them in mind as you climb—the cool sounds of the rushing water help your frame of mind on a hot day. There is little shade on the trail, so pack some liquid along for the higher parts of the climb beyond the creek. Altogether there is a 1980-ft. (600-m) elevation gain on this hike; you will be climbing almost constantly until the top.

Before the trail was upgraded, hikers had to pull themselves up through the roots of the trees that sewed the mountainside together. It's still necessary to scramble over a lot of roots, but they actually form part of the staircase that takes you up. The trail is very well marked, so there is no mistaking direction even if you should find yourself clouded in. During the entire climb you will find yourself walking up, around, next to, and under the solid granite of the Chief.

You leave the creek behind after 20 minutes. The trail divides: the upper left fork goes to the three peaks, 45 to 70 minutes away depending on your route. (The right-hand fork leads up to the Stawamus Squaw, 2 hours distant, a companion peak to the Chief. This is also an alternative route to Third Peak, bypassing the Second Peak trail.) The trail divides again 20 minutes later, just past an enormous boulder perched precariously on a ledge. This is the first opportunity to look out and see how high you've climbed. The rock face is intriguing at this point, a weighty wall of granite streaked with colours from oxidizing minerals. (The interior of the rock, as you can see from the freshly split boulders at the bottom of the Chief, is bright white speckled with black dots.)

The trail is smooth and wide in most places. The higher you get the more exhilarating it becomes until finally, near the top and above the treeline, you reach a very broad and open windswept spot. The most difficult part is now behind you; relax and contemplate the lunch menu on this final section.

From the top you can see Shannon Falls in profile to the south, with the ribbon of Highway 99 curving beyond until it goes out of sight past the Garibaldi viewpoint. To the north, the Squamish River cuts through the valley between Brackendale and Howe Sound. Across the water to the west are the glaciated peaks of the Tantalus Range.

Your imagination may begin to work overtime as you approach the edge of the cliffs. Thinking about the sheer walls below is dizzying and speaks to a deep fear of falling. You may find that your legs tremble involuntarily up on the Chief, as if the earth were moving. Strange, considering that under your feet is one enormous piece of rock. It's a bit of a test of will to get close to the edge as the wind blows over the top. If you're feeling particularly intrepid, have someone hold onto your ankles while you lean over for a look. It's not as dangerous as it feels, but obviously it's best to be cautious, especially with children.

Your descent is buoyed by satisfaction at having made the climb, blended with relief at getting down off the top after all the drama of the Chief. Toes now begin to shove into the front of hiking shoes for the next 90 minutes, so choose socks and footwear accordingly. This hike is an adventure and an accomplishment. You'll never pass the Chief again without remembering that wonderful shaky feeling on top.

STAWAMUS AND MAMQUAM RIVERS   The Stawamus River flows around the north face of the mountain. Driving past the viewpoint of Stawamus Chief Mountain on Highway 99, watch for a gravel road running east on the south side of the Stawamus River. If you'd like a close look at the north face of the Chief take this turn; the road leads uphill for 2 mi. (3.2 km) to a bridge over the Stawamus. A deep cleft splits the face peak to base down the middle. Nearby a rough side road runs up to the Stawamus Squaw. Farther east is a good viewpoint of both

---

SQUAMISH TRANSIT

The Squamish Transit System operates Monday to Saturday, excluding holidays. It also serves Brackendale and Garibaldi Highlands. At present the fare is $1. Buses make the round-trip journey via two routes, the North and South loops, every 80 minutes. There are 11 stops at key locations throughout the district, including the Smoke Bluffs on Vista Crescent. Call 898-9025 for a detailed schedule. Connections can be made with Maverick Coach Lines, which serves Squamish from Vancouver, Whistler, and Pemberton. (In Vancouver, phone 662-8051; in Whistler, 932-5031; in Pemberton, 894-6818.)

mountains from a roadside pull-off. From here you can also look north across the Stawamus River to a low granite ridge named the Smoke Bluffs.

The road now crosses a log bridge spanning the Stawamus River, then divides. The road to the right leads along the river for a short distance before dividing yet again next to several small buildings housing the Squamish water chlorination system. At present you cannot drive beyond here, but if you are on a bike you can explore farther up the Stawamus River on the dike trail that continues on to a small dam. The watershed is closed past this point. The Stawamus River has flooded in the past because of heavy rains, and the north bank is now reinforced with bales of rocks in wire netting. A trail along the top of the dike leads from the dam downstream to Highway 99. It is very loose gravel in places, harder to negotiate than the dirt road past the Squaw and the Chief.

If you wish to explore further in the Stawamus River area, drive or cycle along a hard-packed dirt road leading off to the left across from the chlorination sheds. It is level and runs over to the south bank of the Mamquam River, a 15-minute ride by bike. Near the road's end it divides again. The left fork goes only a short distance farther. From here an old trail runs downhill to the Mamquam. The right fork descends to where a blue pipeline crosses the river. A well-trodden pathway leads along the riverbank to the left, a pleasant 10-minute walk through the forest to several small campsites next to a wide gravel bar. The broad river has too strong a current for swimming, but this is a good place for fishing.

SMOKE BLUFFS   Rock climbing's popularity around Squamish is not limited to the Chief. Close by is the Smoke Bluffs, a small ridge easily reached by road. Because of the ridge's southern exposure, the granite walls dry quickly in the morning sun. Climbers groom the rock face with wire brushes to obtain an ideal smoothness. Over the past few years the Federation of B.C. Mountain Clubs has purchased several adjacent pieces of land, effectively preserving the ridge for recreation. Together with the Squamish Rockclimbers Association and the Squamish Municipal Council, the federation is lobbying to have the 67-acre (27-ha) site with its 200 climbing routes designated as a provincial park. If they're successful, the Smoke Bluffs will become the only park in Canada specifically for rock-climbing.

Finding your way to the Smoke Bluffs is not difficult, and there are several approaches from which to choose. As Highway 99 crests the hill north of the Chief, watch for the intersection sign pointing to Squamish General Hospital. Turn right at the lights then left, and drive past the hospital to the top of Vista Crescent. The small parking area here is posted with a sign prohibiting overnight camping. On summer weekends there are usually more cars than the lot can handle, and the overflow lines Vista in both directions. This is a residential area; while the neighbours appear to be tolerant, they probably don't appreciate picnickers on their front lawns. (Another approach, usually less congested, begins from the parking area beside the Mamquam Blind Channel on Loggers Lane, just east of Highway 99.)

There is a portable outhouse in the parking area and another with a notice board beside the trail leading up to the Smoke Bluffs. The map posted here details the various approaches to the bluffs and shows the locations of several good viewpoints (one of the best is nearby at Pixie Corner).

A series of rough trails leads up to the base of the ridge. Small groups of climbers practise on the smooth walls here. While this isn't a spectator sport, they won't mind you watching if you are quiet; safe climbing requires great concentration. The trail north around the base of the Smoke Bluffs descends onto an open plateau and below to the bank of the Mamquam Blind Channel.

From inside the parking area off Vista Crescent an old road, blocked off to vehicles, runs east through the trees. This is the beginning of a scenic loop trail that climbs through the forest. You can walk it in 30 minutes. Shortly after you begin, you pass a gated road leading down to Plateau Drive. The loop trail bears left past the gate and begins to climb the bluffs. Wood and rock staircases lead up to one section called the Octopus's Garden. Farther along the loop trail narrows as it curves between two granite walls. Watch for wooden stairs leading down to Pixie Corner. The loop trail brings you out at the notice board near Vista Crescent.

(If you follow the road past the gate to Plateau Drive, it leads downhill to the Stawamus River dike trail beside a yellow gate. A gravel road also runs from here up to the bridge over the river. If you are exploring on bike, this makes a good circle route. Go from the Smoke Bluffs to the Stawamus River and cross the bridge, from which point the route is all downhill past the Squaw and the Chief to Highway 99. Turn right onto the highway, cross the bridge over the river, and turn right onto Valley Drive. It will take you back to the bluffs along a smooth section of paved road. Watch for the Sta'a'mus Native Arts and Crafts store on the north side of the Stawamus River beside Highway 99 where Valley Drive begins.)

SQUAMISH MUNICIPAL (BRENNAN PARK) Highway 99 leads north through Squamish to the Mamquam River. Along the way it crosses the Mamquam Blind Channel, a backwater off Howe Sound. Just before the highway crosses the bridge over the Mamquam River you will see an open playing field. Watch for the sign indicating a turnoff to

14

Strong "squamish" winds blow down Howe Sound every day, attracting windsurfers from around the world.

the Forest Service office, located on the east side of the road next to a large playing field. On weekdays you can pick up a copy of the free Squamish Forest District recreation map here. It's also a good place to check current conditions of the back-country roads and bridges and find out about closures because of inclement weather.

The municipality of Squamish maintains lovely Brennan Park adjacent to the Forest Service office. There are also four tennis courts beside the Mamquam River. You can explore the Mamquam on a dike trail, following it to its mouth at the Squamish River. During summer months when water levels are low, there are good sandbars to fish from.

Loggers Lane leads through the park to a group campground for visiting sports teams who come to compete in tournaments. There is also a large community centre with an indoor swimming pool. Loggers Lane runs south for several level miles until it links up with Highway 99 at the top of the Mamquam Blind Channel. The north end of the Smoke Bluffs trail starts here.

SQUAMISH SPIT A strong wind that has come to be known as a "squamish" blows each afternoon, carrying across Howe Sound with such force that unwary windsurfers in the waters off the Squamish Spit often can't right themselves if they get dunked. There is an emergency rescue service available to pluck such hapless types from the waters for a $10 fee which must seem modest to those in need.

The spit is a long finger of dike at the mouth of the Squamish River where it flows into Howe Sound. It was built as a railbed in 1980 in the expectation that coal from Tumbler Ridge in northeastern B.C. would be shipped to freighters in Squamish, on its way to Asian markets; the government decided instead to send the coal via Prince Rupert. The spit helps keep the harbour free of silt so that large freighters can tie up nearby to take on loads of lumber. On busy summer weekends there can be more than a hundred cars parked here. At the very end of the spit is the windsurfer launch area; you can drive to a drop-off point beside it, unload your board, then park if you're here for sport. If you're just here to watch, you can come out by bicycle.

The road to the spit starts off Government Road's west side, just north of the Squamish Valley Feed Supply store. It is 2.7 mi. (4.3 km) along a gravel road from the unmarked turnoff to the end of the spit. Turn left just before the road climbs up on the dike and follow along south to the very end. The surface of the dike is loose gravel, not the best material on which to ride. The spit is administered by the Squamish Windsurfing Society. Launch fees are currently $10 per day or $75 for a season's pass. (For information on daily wind conditions, dial 926-WIND.)

In summer the road is lined with pink Douglas spirea (hardhack), which at a glance can be mistaken for fireweed. The views from the spit are spectacular, the best in the area: Shannon Falls, the Stawamus Chief, Sky Pilot Mountain and Goat Ridge, Mamquam Mountain, Atwell Peak, and Mount Garibaldi all stand out in one great panorama.

2 | DIAMOND HEAD

CAMPING ◄
CYCLING ◄
HIKING ◄
PICNICKING ◄
SNOWSHOEING ◄
VIEWPOINTS ◄
X-C SKIING ◄

Each season brings its own distinct spectrum to the Coast Mountains around Whistler, but autumn is champion in the colour category. The onset of cooler overnight weather starts a magical process in motion, and the first good frost triggers the greens of summer into a slow fade. As photosynthesis shuts down, previously hidden sugars in the plant leaves sweeten the scenery with shades of red, gold, and purple.

When it comes to viewing fall colours around Whistler you have two options: wait for temperatures to dip towards freezing in the valley, or head up a nearby mountain. For recorded weather reports on Whistler Mountain, call 687-6761 in Vancouver or 932-3434 in Whistler; for Blackcomb, dial 687-7507 (Vancouver) or 932-4211. You can also call Environment Canada in Vancouver at 664-9010. They'll help you easily determine the elevation at which frost has begun to occur. The Whistler area begins to experience cool overnight temperatures in September, the best time to catch plants in full blaze. The only thing missing will be the bugs—thank the frost for that, too.

Stands of ash, cottonwood and vine maple flank much of Highway 99, from Howe Sound to the Pemberton Valley, and outline nearby rivers and lakes. Their leaves turn at a much slower pace than those in the alpine regions. Altitude also plays a great part in determining growth patterns. At higher levels the large stands of tall trees give way to smaller, more sporadic groves, and low-lying shrubs thickly carpet the gullies near the peaks. This is where you want to be.

DIAMOND HEAD One of the most easily accessible subalpine regions lies in Garibaldi Provincial Park's southwest corner. Diamond Head is a fortress-like ridge that rises above the Cheakamus River Valley. Accompanied by craggy Atwell Peak, Diamond Head makes a bold statement about the height of the range here. As you travel north of Squamish on

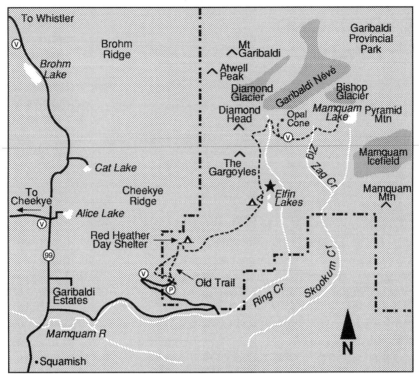

Diamond Head

Highway 99, look straight ahead and up: these two imposing features dwarf all else on the skyline.

You'll be surprised at how quickly you can get a close look at them. Take the exit marked "Diamond Head (Garibaldi Park)" east from Highway 99. One of the pleasures of visiting Diamond Head is this access road; it lets you do much of the initial climbing by car, running 10 miles (16 km) east to the parking lot at the trailhead. The first 2.5 mi. (4 km) is paved, passing through the southern outskirts of Garibaldi Estates. The remaining distance is along Mamquam Road (on a good gravel surface), which climbs gradually above the Mamquam River Valley. The mountainside rises steeply, and dense stands of second-growth forest conceal the view on both sides. Once you've left Highway 99, you won't catch sight of the peaks again until you're walking the Diamond Head trail.

At the 7.5 mi. (12 km) mark the road divides. A large sign points left towards the park boundary. A notice next to it reminds visitors that pets are not permitted in Garibaldi Provincial Park, of which this part is the Black Tusk Nature Conservancy Area. The final 2.5 mi.(4 km) of road covers a series of switchbacks. Only at the last one does the view of the Squamish Valley open up. This is a good place to stop and look south to

18

Howe Sound and Stawamus Chief Mountain peak. Across the valley to the west is Cloudburst Mountain and to the south of it the broad body of glaciers around Mount Tantalus. In the open woods just above this viewpoint are the last remnants of several old cabins.

ELFIN LAKES TRAIL   There is a large map of the Diamond Head region at the trailhead. From the parking lot to the subalpine region is a 6.8-mile (11-km) hike along an old access road. Because the grade is gentle for most of the road, you should be able to reach the Elfin Lakes in 2¹/₂ hours if you are reasonably fit. The map at the trailhead gives a longer estimate of 4 hours. Not many people know that you can journey into this region of Garibaldi on bicycle. While it won't cut much time off your ascent, coming down will take less than an hour.

In the first 15 minutes of your walk to Diamond Head you will see a well-blazed trail leading uphill on your right. This is the original route, and you can cut almost 2 mi. (3 km) off the total distance by taking it. It is steeper going than the road, but you may find the pleasure of climbing through a large stand of Douglas fir compensates for the extra effort. As well, several species of amanita mushrooms seem determined to set new growth records in late summer and early fall, pushing their brown, white or speckled red and yellow tops up beside the forest path. (Caution: most amanitas are very poisonous—if you're hiking with children, watch that they don't touch or eat any mushrooms that you can't positively identify as safe.)

In 45 minutes you will rejoin the road just as the first great views of Diamond Head open up to the north. By now you have entered the subalpine region. Signs indicate where the Ministry of Parks is taking steps to control erosion caused by runoff. Please stick to the trail in these sections.

Red Heather Meadow, with its picnic and day shelter, provides a resting place after 90 minutes on the road. Only in fall and winter will you be safe from the no-see-ums (small biting flies) that call this area home; at other times, come prepared to combat them. As the road rises above Red Heather Meadow the forest thins to groves of cypress trees. These trees are deceptively small, but ring samples indicate that the mature trees are at least 300 years old, and some are twice that. They appear much younger because the growing period here is shorter than in the valley; snowstorms can occur as late as June and resume again in August.

As you near the Elfin Lakes, the road levels as it reaches a ridge; more than anywhere else in the Whistler region, this will remind you of a back road in the Swiss Alps. Unlike most forest company roads, it does not pass through logged areas. Well worn by many bootprints, the road climbs up the mountain in rhythm with the contour of the slope, and walking it is a pleasure.

At any season, the closer you get to Diamond Head, the more colours

The old chalet at Elfin Lakes overlooks Diamond Head ridge with Mount Atwell above.

reveal themselves. What appeared at a distance as dull grey now becomes sandy brown, deep auburn, green, yellow, white and volcanic black. The rippled surface of Diamond Head's sweeping ridge has been deeply grooved by the retreating glacier that still holds sway on the upper slopes.

The Elfin Lakes present themselves suddenly, as the road makes its final descent towards an old chalet. When my family and I first wandered along here, we wondered who had built this smooth approach into the park. It didn't appear to be a logging road as there was no evidence of stumps. (You can easily tell when you have entered Garibaldi park by the girth of the old-growth Douglas firs.) When we arrived on top, we found the answer.

In the 1940s, a remarkable young woman from West Vancouver named Joan Matthews and two brothers from Norway, Ottar and Emil Brandvold, built a log house they called the Diamond Head Chalet in these subalpine meadows. The old road was the approach that introduced people to these mountains over the past half-century. Joan left in the late 1950s, and the brothers operated the chalet for another decade of visitors after it was sold to the province for the park. The balsam-log structure now stands boarded up; had it been built with harder wood, it might serve for more than storage today. From the outside, though, it is still invested with the wealth of charm that characterizes many of the lodges farther north around Alta Lake.

JOAN MATTHEWS

Joan Matthews was born in West Vancouver in 1920, the grand-daughter of Henry Stone, who was among the original settlers of West Vancouver and a founder of the Vancouver School of Art. Joan was a sculptor by training, one of several women in the first graduating class of the Vancouver Art College in 1942.

Active in winter sports as a teenager, she became a champion slalom skier in the 1930s. In the late '30s Joan built herself a cabin on Hollyburn Ridge overlooking Vancouver. During World War II she worked in the summer, and in winter mapped out ski routes on Black Mountain and in the back country north of Squamish. At a ski meet in Wells Gray Park she met two world-class Norwegian ski jumpers, Ottar and Emil Brandvold, who then stayed on as war refugees. She introduced them to the Whistler region and in 1942 married Ottar. The three built the chalet at Diamond Head in 1945-46.

Matthews is remembered by her friend Rose Tatlow as being the driving force behind the Diamond Head project. Joan negotiated the land rights with the provincial government, and worked shoulder to shoulder with the two soft-spoken brothers while displaying the constant cheerfulness that was her hallmark.

In 1975 the Ministry of Parks, which has administered Garibaldi park since its inception in 1920, built a Panabode cabin next to the old lodge. There is bunkbed accommodation for up to 30 visitors at a cost of $10 each per night. It's quite cozy inside, a favourite nest for nordic skiers on cold winter nights. As well, the parks department has made a special effort to serve the needs of seniors. For those over 60 who would like to spend a night or two in the chalet without having to pack food with them, arrangements can be made for modest meals. Gizelde Behin, a woman of Norwegian heritage and a longtime friend of the Brandvolds, is often in residence. She prepares three meals a day at a charge of $4 each. To find out if she is cooking, call her at 926-4425.

The Elfin Lakes are really little more than two alpine ponds. One is reserved solely for drinking water, the other for washing. Several picnic tables sit on the open slope next to a small interpretive display. The history of the region is explained simply on several laminated panels, complete with archival photos from Joan, Ottar, and Emil's early years here.

In an open meadow just past the Panabode cabin is a large campsite. Although it does not offer much seclusion, there is plenty of room to

Signs of the retreating glaciers are everywhere around the Opal Cone.

spread out. Washroom facilities are nearby. This is as far as you are allowed to cycle. Your next stage is on foot, at first in the tracks of an old wagon road.

BEYOND ELFIN LAKES The fall colours here are certainly not confined to trees. The ground cover of red heather interwoven with low-lying blueberry bushes is a riot of scarlets. Six shades of yellow, from gold to pumpkin, climb the banks of small gullies to where scree has tumbled down from the eroding cones of the ancient volcanoes characteristic of the region. You can walk the trail for hours more beyond Elfin Lakes, limited only by the remaining light, the weather, and the extent of your preparations.

Even if you don't feel like walking much past the lakes, do take 15 minutes to catch a brief glimpse of this continually changing landscape. Some of the most vivid colouring occurs in the gullies on the first part of the trail, which eventually leads to distant Mamquam Lake. The Opal Cone, an interesting remnant of an old volcanic rim, is 2 hours' hike away from the Elfin Lakes along this trail.

At first much of the trail to the Opal Cone is downhill. Views of the Gargoyles, gnarled black rock formations hulking on Diamond Head's south flank, soon appear. As well, Mount Garibaldi and the Sharkfin begin to show their profiles north of Atwell Peak. Across the valley to the east, an enormous sheet of glacial ice hangs on the slopes of Mamquam Mountain. There seems to be more wildlife along this section. Marmots and pikas sunbathe on rocky outcroppings. If you stop to pick blueberries, you'll probably scare up the occasional grouse.

Past the halfway point, where a small bridge crosses boulder-strewn, silt-grey, glacier-fed Ring Creek, you enter a barren landscape. Walking here is harder because of rock debris recently deposited by the retreating glacier. Perhaps in another century plants will take root, giving fall a chance to colour these slopes, too.

The trail climbs towards the ridge beside the Opal Cone. If you only want a view of this ancient volcano, bear left where the trail divides. After 30 minutes on this steep trail you will reach a viewpoint of the Opal Cone and the icefields spread below Mount Garibaldi. If your destination is Mamquam Lake, bear right at the point where the trail divides. The lake is several hours' walk east of the Opal Cone.

3 | SQUAMISH AND PARADISE VALLEYS

The back roads from Squamish north to Brackendale are easy routes on which to walk or pedal. You can choose to follow a gentle country road or a river dike trail; neither is lengthy or vertically challenging. The farms you pass along the way are perhaps small compared to the wide expanse of the Pemberton prairie to the north, but good places nevertheless to stretch your legs while enjoying seasonal colours, counting eagles, and retracing pioneer byways. The finest hops in the British Empire were once grown here and exported to England for use in brewing beer. A reminder of this former glory is preserved in the name Hop Ranch Creek (also known as Hog Ranch Creek).

The region is dominated by four rivers that converge into one just before meeting the ocean. The Cheakamus River, having almost completed its flow south from Whistler, picks up water from the Cheekye just prior to joining the Squamish near Brackendale. The Mamquam River comes in from the east to add volume to the Squamish downstream from Brackendale. Small wonder that a large dike stands ready in case of a sudden rise in water levels.

As you come north on Buckley Street it turns into Government Road after crossing the B.C. Rail tracks. The railway is a major employer locally. A large repair yard is located on the east side of Government Road. Opposite it is the new home of the B.C. Railway Museum.

BRACKENDALE　European settlers began arriving in the Squamish Valley in the late 1880s. The first homes were built in the Brackendale area; it was not until the turn of the century that the town of Squamish came into existence on the site of a hayfield. (According to Squamish pioneer Rose Tatlow, the oldest house still standing in the valley is the one built by Alfred Barnfield at the southwest corner of Buckley and Wilson Crescent on the way from Squamish to Brackendale. Barnfield was one of the first to begin referring informally to the peak above Alta

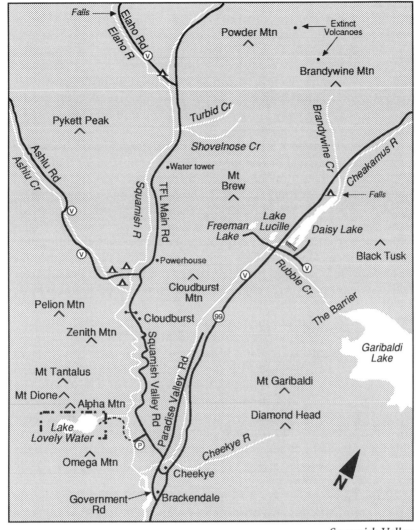

Squamish Valley

Lake as Whistler Mountain, apparently because early visitors noticed large numbers of whistling marmots on the slopes of what was then called London Mountain.) Most of the early homes were modest cabins. An exception to this is the lovely two-storey Judd house, on Judd Road west of Government. It stands on a large lot surrounded by an ancient orchard. Nearby is the Armstrong house at 40215 Government Road, home to the first white child born in the valley.

Once an important relay station on the Pemberton Trail, Brackendale was eclipsed by Squamish when the port began to grow in importance as logging supplanted farming as the main occupation. Today Brackendale is beginning to resemble a bedroom community of Squamish. Although it's only 4.6 mi. (7.5 km) north of Squamish, it sometimes took early travellers a half-day to make the journey between the two. It's difficult to imagine such hardship as you speed along Highway 99, covering the distance in mere minutes. The wide paved shoulders on each side of the highway make for easy riding if you come this way by bike.

Brackendale has been home to a large population of bald eagles since long before the arrival of Europeans. Each year in January there is an annual tally of their numbers. In 1988 there were 2,542 eagles counted along the Squamish River, one of the largest nesting colonies of these magnificent birds in North America. When the tall black cottonwoods stand bare you can see massive nests high in their branches. Eagles return each year to reclaim these penthouses, repairing and adding new material to them. One of the best viewing spots is from the top of the dike beside Government Road directly across from the Easter Seals Camp. You may see as many as 30 eagles at any one time. (The Squamish River didn't always flow this close. Longtime residents remember when hayfields stretched a half-mile west of where the dike stands. This land was inundated when the river assumed its present channel.)

The Brackendale Art Gallery, Theatre and Teahouse on Government Road just north of Depot Road makes a good stop on the way through town. Open weekends and holidays from noon to 10 PM, it hosts a variety of artistic, musical, and dramatic productions throughout the year. (Phone 898-3332 for details on current productions.) Sculptor Thor Froslev, who began building this sprawling space in 1969, is also responsible for publicizing Brackendale as the winter home of the bald eagle. The distinctive wooden sign on Highway 99, dominated by the profile of an eagle, is his creation.

Across Government Road from the gallery is the old Brackendale general store, cafe and post office, where many cyclists stop to enjoy ice cream while admiring the large mural of the surrounding mountainscape. The store was preceded by an even older relay station, the only remaining sign of which is the blackened chimney in a field beside Government Road across from the cafe. (In the 1880s William Shannon began a brickyard below the falls that now bear his name; bricks for this chimney and others still standing in the area were made from the rich clay deposits at the mouth of Shannon Creek.)

Just north of Brackendale on Government Road is a small airfield out of which Glacier Air flies. There are a number of tours from which to choose. You can charter a five-passenger plane for a 30-minute flight at a cost of $125 to fly over any part of the region that appeals to you. You might not otherwise have an opportunity to view the small lakes inlaid between the peaks and icefields of the Tantalus Range, a truly memorable experience. Glacier Air's phone number is 898-9016 (683-0209 from Vancouver, 932-2705 from Whistler).

Just north of Brackendale, Government Road meets the Squamish Valley Road coming west from Highway 99. Signs on Highway 99 indicate the turnoff to Squamish and Paradise valleys. Just as you begin driving west from 99 towards the small native Indian settlement of Cheekye, one of the best views of Atwell Peak, Dalton Dome and the red lava ridge below them rises in the east. Take a moment to look that way, especially late in the day when the sun lights up the rock face. A bridge crosses the Cheakamus River at Cheekye, and on its far side the road divides into the Squamish Valley Road to the left, and the Paradise Valley Road to the right. If you'd like to explore this area on horseback, call Cheekye Stables (898-3432), located on the Squamish Valley Road 1 mi.(1.6 km) east of Cheekye.

SQUAMISH VALLEY ROAD   Floods occur in the Squamish Valley with predictable frequency. The most recent was in August 1991, when the Cheakamus River overflowed its banks beside the settlement of Cheekye, turning roadbeds into gravel bars. Recovering from natural disasters takes time; the cycle of destruction and improvement keeps residents busy. It also keeps visitors at bay. Until the road is repaired even trucks and 4x4s will be rattled when travelling up either Squamish or Paradise valleys north of Cheekye.

The rewards for making the journey up the Squamish Valley are manifold. Glaciers robe the slopes of the Tantalus Range. The wide river welcomes paddlers. Sandbars make for soft campsites.

Partnered with the prosaically named TFL Main (for "Tree Farm Licence"), the Squamish Valley Road runs northwest for a combined total of 25 mi. (40 km). It's intermittently gravelled and paved as it winds through shady stands of maple towards a small settlement informally known as Cloudburst. The Squamish River accompanies the road in places but is hidden for the most part. When improvements to the flood-damaged sections have been completed this will once again be a good place to cycle. There's a particularly good viewpoint of Mount Tantalus from the one-lane bridge across Pillchuck Creek.

The valley is a narrow flood plain, with hardly a cleared space. The occasional home sits atop large raised earthen pads or on stilt supports. A good example is just off the main road at Cloudburst Farm, where there are fresh vegetables for sale in summer; the main house and all of the outbuildings stand on solid pilings. Insurance against most natural calamities is impossible to come by, and the provincial government no longer bails out valley residents after a deluge. Thus only the brave (or foolhardy) are tempted to build here. But those who do have a view of

Looking up at Mount Tantalus from the Squamish Valley.

Mount Tantalus and its companion peaks that beats any other hands down. A tantalus is a stand on which crystal decanters are displayed, and Mount Tantalus certainly displays the frozen crystals on its slopes to best advantage. (Tantalus was also the name of a mythological Greek king; the names of adjacent peaks such as Alpha and Omega also reflect the Greek influence.)

Much of the first 11.8 mi. (19 km) passes through a series of Indian reserves. You will notice many signs advising that reserve land is private. Visitors are allowed access with permission from the Squamish Indian Band Council (985-7111). This is important if you intend to hike up to the recreation area at Lake Lovely Water, one of B.C.'s newest provincial parks.

LAKE LOVELY WATER   Who could resist visiting a recreation area with such an appealing name? The only hitch is that in order to reach it you must paddle across the Squamish River and then hike 4 hours up a steep trail with hardly a view to recommend it until you are at lakeside. But what a lakeside, cradled between the peaks of Alpha and Omega mountains. After all the effort you expend reaching the lake, you may wish to camp. The Alpine Club of Canada maintains a locked cabin beside the lake. You can make arrangements to get the key if you call in advance (737-3053); there is a modest fee for non-members. Otherwise pack along a tent.

Pick up the route to the lake exactly 1.2 mi. (2 km) to the left off the Squamish Valley Road from the Cheekye bridge. Drive a short distance along this rough but passable road to a water-gauging station beside the Squamish River. Park here. Launch your boat where you can (careful of the current at times of high water), and head to a point just north of the wooden tower on the opposite bank. Do not attempt to use the cable car strung between the two towers. When the water is low, you can pull your boat up at one of several small clearings on the shore. Tie up the boat securely and stash your paddles in the underbrush. You want them to be waiting on your return.

The trail to Lake Lovely Water is an old one. In order to find it, begin walking north along the riverbank. Watch for surveyor's tape tied to branches and metal disks nailed to trees. This is as reliable as the marking gets. Stay on the riverbank trail for 30 minutes. When you arrive at a boulder-filled creekbed, dry in summer months and not too mossy, begin climbing. It will take you 10 minutes of difficult scrambling over the boulders to find the trail that begins to follow the eroded creekbed's south side; once on it, the marking improves. From here to the lake takes 3 hours. Along the way you pass through dense stands of original-growth forest and cross several small creeks and the occasional rockslide. Lovelywater Creek drains a long distance down the mountain from the lake. You only get close enough to it to admire its whitewater. Through the branches you may catch sight of the Black Tusk once you achieve altitude.

One of the steepest sections is right at the top. It helps to keep reminding yourself that pain is but a sharp sauce to the dish of pleasure. And what a pleasure it is to reach the lake—but what pain when you see a floatplane touch down effortlessly on its turquoise surface, depositing a party of fishermen or hikers here for the afternoon. On reflection, perhaps this is the better way to go. The price of a round-trip ride for a party of five is the equivalent of a day's skiing at Whistler. Treat yourself.

TFL MAIN   Just past the farmyards of Cloudburst (watch for cattle on the road) is the gateway to Tree Farm 38, operated by Weldwood of Canada. The logging company controls access from here north into the valley. Public traffic is usually permitted after hours on weekdays and all day on weekends and holidays. It's best to be cautious, keep right, and drive with your headlights on at all times.

The Squamish Valley and the river widen for the next 12.4 mi. (20 km). By August, when water levels have usually dropped to their seasonal lows, sandbars appear and provide excellent picnicking, camping and fishing locations. Dolly Varden char and cutthroat trout run in the silty grey Squamish, water that never really warms up enough for more than a quick plunge, even on the hottest days.

ASHLU CREEK   Soon after passing the Weldwood gate you'll come to a bridge that crosses the river near its confluence with Ashlu Creek. There are natural picnic and camping spots on the far side. Ashlu Creek is one of the few major tributaries feeding the Squamish from the west. A short distance along the Ashlu road is another bridge, near the "Mile 22" sign. There are several more campsites on the small delta here. The open ground is composed of very fine sand, making for gentle walking, a good play area for children, and a safe place for campfires. When water levels are low in Ashlu Creek, you can wade upstream to admire the scenery.

From here to a bridge at "Mile 25" the road climbs through Ashlu Canyon, with several good viewpoints along the way, especially between miles 23 and 24. Ashlu Creek carves its way through the rock here with deadly force. The road climbs for a long way beyond the canyon without encountering anything else as visually stimulating. Clouds from the ocean waters of Jervis Inlet to the west of Ashlu Creek often vent like steam over the slopes of Mount Jimmy Jimmy into the headwaters of the creek.

30

Water surges through Ashlu Canyon.

ELAHO RIVER   Granite walls rise above the east side of the Squamish River, forcing the TFL Main to hug its slopes as it heads north of the Ashlu Creek bridge turnoff. You soon pass the Cheakamus Powerhouse, which receives water pumped through a tunnel from Daisy Lake—a reminder of how interconnected this valley is with Whistler.

There are often cars parked near a water tower north of the power-house, waiting for owners who are out paddling or hiking. This is a good spot from which to launch a raft, kayak, or canoe. In summer the current in the Squamish is often conducive to a leisurely paddle downstream. If you're travelling with a group you can leave one vehicle at the tower and another at one of several locations along Government Road or even at the Squamish Spit, waiting for you when you decide to pull out of the

31

FIRE AND ICE

Twelve thousand years ago the Pleistocene epoch, which had held most of North America in an intermittent state of icy shock for more than 500,000 years, came to an end and the glaciers began to withdraw. After covering our local mountains from valley to peak, the huge glaciers slowly wore most of them down to stubs during their retreat. The ice age was a sore loser. If it couldn't keep the peaks, it wasn't about to leave the Coast Mountains for any inheritors to admire. But just when it appeared that the local topography would have all the excitement of a soda cracker, up popped lava-spewing volcanoes. What nature had nearly eradicated in one glacial impulse, it rebuilt in a molten moment. Once their work was done, the volcanoes sealed up. The remnants of the icefields, stranded at high altitudes, slowly carried on their meltdown. These glaciers are still with us today, and should see us through the next several centuries—a blink in time, geologically, but an important link to an earlier eon.

river. Drive back with a partner to reclaim the vehicle you left by the water tower.

While hundreds of small glacier-fed waterfalls pour off the mountain on the western side of the valley, Mount Brew rises unseen above the road to the east. The silty waters of Shovelnose and Turbid creeks, coming down off the slopes of Brandywine Mountain, pass beneath the road as it nears the northern end of the valley. Here at last, a half-hour drive from the Weldwood gate, are the best spots for picnicking and camping on the Squamish. A bridge leads across the Squamish next to where it meets the Elaho River. Check from the bridge for a good spot to park and spread out. A short distance up the Elaho road on the left is an old road leading down to the site of two bridges that once spanned the Elaho.

The Elaho road climbs in dramatic contrast to the level 25 mi. (40 km) you've just travelled. Looking down into the canyon of the Elaho River, you can understand how it comes by its reputation as a widowmaker. One mistake in a raft or kayak and you could be in serious trouble. The road continues to climb above the canyon until it passes over Maude Frickert Creek, then enters a long level valley. The creek creates a waterfall as it cascades down, showering the road with spray. Stop here for a bit and let nature wash the dust off your car.

The most interesting part of your journey is behind you now. Heavy-handed logging has cleared the forest right to the banks of the Elaho in places, accounting for much of the debris that jams up in the canyon—

and the scarcity of wildlife, which once thrived here. Only the moose in a protected herd farther up the valley have been spared.

Look for a picnic spot on the riverside. You will have to do some scrambling over and around the detritus in order to make your way to the river. Beside its banks you can relax and momentarily put the ravaged site out of your mind. To the northwest are the glaciers of Mount Ralph, which feed the Elaho. Over the icy peaks to the west, a short distance by air, is Princess Louisa Inlet. To the north the Pemberton Icefield leads up towards Mount Meager. Looking back to the east, you can finally see the glaciers of the Pacific Ranges on the tops of Callaghan, Powder, and Brandywine mountains—three of the extinct volcanoes that moulded this region.

PARADISE VALLEY Paradise Valley is a narrow stretch of land carved out by the Cheakamus River, flanked by high ridges on either side. Highway 99 climbs above the valley to the east; a series of small lakes lies hidden from view on the west side. The B.C. Rail line also charts a careful course through here. Less than half the length of nearby Squamish Valley, Paradise has a quiet flavour of its own. (See Cat and Brohm Lakes chapter for map of this area.)

If you take the right-hand road from the bridge at Cheekye, you will be travelling on the Paradise Valley Road. It used to be paved for a third of its 9.3-mi. (15-km) length. Since the August 1991 flood, conditions have deteriorated considerably. You'll just have to take it easy. The rewards for making the journey are several good picnic and fishing spots on the banks of the Cheakamus River. The road beside the river at the north end of the valley is part of the old Pemberton Trail.

Soon after beginning your drive north on the Paradise Valley Road you pass by the North Vancouver Outdoor School. Students learn about the environment during their stays. A conference centre is available for use by other groups during summer months (phone 980-5116). The land on which the outdoor school stands was homesteaded by Jim Levette. He named Paradise Valley and gave his name to a nearby lake. Several old fruit trees from his orchard still flourish on the school's grounds. Signs of the Pemberton Trail can be seen on the scree across the road from the school.

Directly across the road from the school is a road leading up to Evans, Levette, and Hut lakes. While Evans is a private lake and Hut is inaccessible to all but the hardiest 4x4 drivers or fishermen who opt to hike in, Levette has a public side to it. The 2.5-mi. (4-km) road to Levette can be rough and tricky, especially as it climbs the last section before reaching the shore. A trail runs around the lake with several open spots for picnicking. The bottom drops off quickly; you can swim in the warm waters from logs or launch small hand-carried boats. Views of Omega

The major highway viewpoints above Paradise Valley offer a panorama of the Tantalus Range.

Mountain to the west, hidden by the forest at lakeside, are the reward for making the effort to get out on the lake. For cyclists who have come up from Squamish, reaching Levette Lake is the crowning accomplishment to a day trip. There are several primitive campsites beside the lake and an outhouse nearby. The lake is popular on weekends, despite its modest stature.

The Paradise Valley Road crosses the Cheakamus River just north of the outdoor school. The Tenderfoot Fish Hatchery is at the south end of a short stretch of the road called Midnight Way. The Paradise Valley Road crosses the B.C. Rail tracks at each end of Midnight Way. It's possible to drive north for another 6.8 mi. (11 km). The best riverbank spots occur after the road crosses Culliton Creek on the "Jack Webster" bridge. (The name of this Vancouver broadcaster was painted on the side of the bridge during flooding in 1984.) Watch for postings advising of fishing closures during the spring. The river is turquoise-green and frigid, even in the dog days of August.

The rock walls on each side of the Cheakamus River close in at the north end of Paradise Valley. The old Pemberton Trail once led travellers past here up one of its steepest parts to Bear Mountain. Signs of the trail are still evident today, although the road is recommended for 4x4 traffic only. Cyclists will find that the rocky road climbs too steeply to maintain traction for long. You'll have to dismount and push for much of the way. But you can get some good views of the Cheakamus Canyon if you walk along the road for a bit to where it intersects with the railway. If you are infused with energy, continue north along the BCR tracks, which lead into the canyon. The views from here are even better, but pay close attention for the sound of trains, and leave yourself plenty of room to stand aside.

If you wish to try this section of the Pemberton Trail on a mountain bike, consider beginning from the second Tantalus viewpoint (where the road opens up after an especially twisty section) on the west side of Highway 99. The very rough trail begins just south of the cement retaining barrier and descends 6.2 mi. (10 km) into Paradise Valley. (This stretch is part of the annual autumn Cheakamus Challenge mountain-bike race, which begins in Paradise Valley and ends at Whistler.) Arrange to be picked up farther down towards Squamish. This makes a good day trip.

4 | ALICE LAKE PROVINCIAL PARK

CAMPING ◄
CYCLING ◄
FISHING ◄
HIKING ◄
PADDLING ◄
PICNICKING ◄
SWIMMING ◄
VIEWPOINTS ◄
WALKING ◄

Warm freshwater lakes are as delightful a discovery as you can make when exploring the countryside around Whistler. Alice Lake is the largest of four tightly knit lakes nestled in the Squamish Valley, 7.4 mi. (12 km) from Squamish. Established as a provincial park in 1956, Alice Lake was named for the wife of pioneer logger Charlie Rose. The Roses were among the first settlers to arrive in the Brackendale region in the 1880s. They homesteaded the land on which the park is located.

This park can be extremely deceiving to first-time visitors. I made my first stop at Alice Lake several years ago with my family, on the return leg of a journey much farther up Highway 99. Tired of fighting traffic, we drove into the picnic area for a brief respite. Having just spent a weekend camped beside a roaring creek in the wilderness, we found the sight of groomed lawns gently rolling down to the shore of Alice Lake unnerving. We paused long enough to refresh ourselves, then headed for home. After that I thought of Alice Lake as a suburban retreat for those who feel somewhat squeamish about what lies hidden under the veneer of civilization.

When we finally returned to explore the park in depth, it was because I needed a place to stretch my legs while getting my feet accustomed to a new pair of hiking boots. I thought we might be able to climb up on the ridge above the park for a look out over the valley. What I discovered was that this is a spectacular part of the Squamish region, with views of Howe Sound, the Tantalus glaciers, and the Cheakamus River as it cuts its way through a granite gorge.

ALICE LAKE Signs near the park entry direct visitors to Alice Lake, where there are day-use facilities as well as 88 campsites (the charge for use is $13 per night, May to October). Of the four lakes in the park, Alice is the one most suitable for paddling (motorized boats are not permitted on any of the lakes). There are launch sites at each end of the lake beside the picnic areas. Rows of tables ring the shore, each with its own

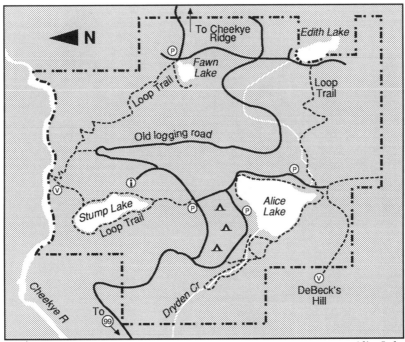

Alice Lake

barbecue. The setting, with its manicured tranquillity, is quite pleasant. There is a pier to fish from at the south end. Lakeshore Walk links the two picnic areas, shaded by cedar groves that thrive on the moisture provided by the lake. The view from Alice Lake's north end is one of the best in the park, short of climbing nearby DeBeck's Hill.

FOUR LAKES LOOP TRAIL   If you are visiting for the day you don't necessarily have to leave your car at Alice Lake. Once in the park, take the left turn towards the park headquarters. You will almost immediately see space for several cars at the beginning of the trail that links all four lakes within the park (Alice, Stump, Fawn, and Edith lakes). There is a public telephone next to the trailhead.

Plan on 2 to 4 hours to complete the round-trip, depending on how many stops you wish to make along the way. All of the trails are well marked, with both directions and distances indicated. From this parking area the distance to Stump Lake is 0.2 mi (0.3 km); to Fawn Lake 1.4 mi. (2.3 km); to Edith Lake 2.2 mi. (3.5 km). This is a fun trail for cycling, one of the activities encouraged year-round in the park.

Begin by walking the short distance to Stump Lake. The name conjures up images of decrepitude, so it's a pleasant surprise to discover that the only stumps in sight stand beside the trail, not in the lake itself.

The serenity of Alice Lake makes it ideal for small boats.

Because it was logged over several decades before being made into a park, the area has some impressively wide stumps.

The smooth trail divides as it rounds the small lake. On one side it's quite level; on the other it climbs the hillside. Looking down you may see fishermen casting for rainbow, cutthroat and brook trout. In contrast to Alice, there are no lawns or beaches here or at either of the next two lakes. Instead there is the occasional blow-down on which you can walk out from the shore to see skunk cabbage blooming beside water lilies, with Alice Ridge high above. To the north Atwell Peak and Mount Garibaldi are visible.

From Stump Lake's north end the trail winds close beside the Cheekye River for a time, then begins to climb gently towards Fawn Lake. The forest floor is thick with ferns; beside the trail delicate wild-flowers such as white trilliums and dusky-rose bleeding hearts appear in clusters. Beneath several large old-growth cedars is an especially pretty viewpoint overlooking the river. (If you are walking with young children, this may be as far as you care to go on the Four Lakes Loop trail. Instead of continuing farther you can take a short connector to an old logging road that leads back to Alice Lake.)

The trail to Fawn Lake gradually climbs away from the Cheekye River, leaving the sounds of rushing water for the silence of the forest and an occasional bird call. In the 20 to 30 minutes it takes to reach Fawn Lake, there's time to listen to the sound of your own thoughts.

Fawn Lake is smaller and shallower, with a shoreline less accessible than those of Stump or Alice lakes. It's possible to swim from the banks of a small clearing. This is exactly what many cyclists do after a long ride uphill on the old road. The warm water is alive with activity as little tadpoles fidget around below the surface. A rough trail attempts to circle the lake before disappearing in a shallow, marshy section. The surrounding woods are surprisingly open in places, with little undergrowth except for a deep moss carpet covering the forest floor.

A former logging road and the Four Lakes Loop trail merge for the short 10- to 15-minute walk between Fawn and Edith lakes. The road is lined with old trees, the sound of the wind high in their branches. An occasional train whistle rises from the valley below. Ravens fly by, the *whoosh* of their beating wings resembling an owl's hoot.

From Edith Lake's north end there are good views of Goat Ridge and other snowy slopes in the distance. While there is one rough approach to the lake from the road, most of the waterfront is not within the park boundary. Several private cottages have the lake mostly to themselves. From here an obscure road leads out of the park and down into Garibaldi Highlands, 2.5 mi. (4 km) away.

The turnoff from the road to the Alice Lake section of the trail is well marked. This leg takes 20 minutes to complete. At midpoint there are some steep stretches as it keeps company with a small creek flowing from Edith to Alice. Simple wooden bridges span the creek in several places. Close to where the creek spills out into Alice Lake, a charming little stone channel has been built into the hillside to carry the water this final distance.

DEBECK'S HILL   If you still have some stamina, try tackling DeBeck's Hill, an option that presents itself at Alice Lake's south end. The hill appears on the detailed park map, but there are no signs indicating the approach, simply a large yellow gate barring vehicles from the road, which climbs relentlessly uphill. A clearing, in which firewood for the campsites lies mounded, appears near the start. Plan on taking 30 minutes to reach the top of the hill.

Just before reaching the summit, you will pass beside an old logging donkey sitting high on its log skids. The smell of grease still hangs in the

This "steam donkey" on DeBeck's Hill above Alice Lake is a relic of early logging days.

air, 30 years after it was last used. By contrast, at the very top of the hill is an ultramodern microwave relay station.

During some seasons you may find yourself fending off the persistent attention of bugs. A cool breeze usually blows across the top of DeBeck's Hill; the insects disappear as quickly as the panoramic views appear. You'll get the complete picture of local geography from up here.

5 | CAT AND BROHM LAKES

CAMPING ◄
CYCLING ◄
FISHING ◄
PADDLING ◄
PICNICKING ◄
SWIMMING ◄
WALKING ◄

As Highway 99 begins to climb above Paradise Valley north of Brackendale, it passes between two small lakes named Cat and Brohm. The Forest Service maintains them as recreation sites. They attract many visitors in warm months, especially older teenagers, and are left almost entirely undisturbed in other seasons. During daylight hours the warm water in these lakes is the number-one attraction. When the scent of summer is in the air, both lakes can count on hosting informal grad parties on their shores. Unless you're in the mood to celebrate through the night, you would be wise to have an alternative campsite in mind.

Cat and Brohm lakes can be an hour's break from the traffic or a destination in themselves. Like all great swimming holes, they are completely satisfying the first moment you jump in. They are also two of the warmest lakes in this region.

CAT LAKE   This sweet little lake has managed to maintain its charm despite years of logging nearby. Its clear, deep waters may hold fish. For sure they once held a fortune in beer bottles. A crew of local skindivers cleaned up the bottom several years ago and financed a trip for themselves to a more exotic climate with the proceeds.

There are a number of campsites spread out around the lake. The road ends next to the best ones, where a small beach serves the needs of young children and non-swimmers. There are few shallow approaches elsewhere on the shore. Several large docks are tethered in strategic places. Some of these are stationary while others can be paddled out into the sunshine. They make good diving platforms. One floats beside a tall tree overhanging the lake; a rope suspended from the branches provides the thrill of swinging out over the lake before releasing and plunging in.

The Cat Lake turnoff from Highway 99 is not marked. It's easiest to find when you are heading north of Alice Lake Provincial Park. Shortly

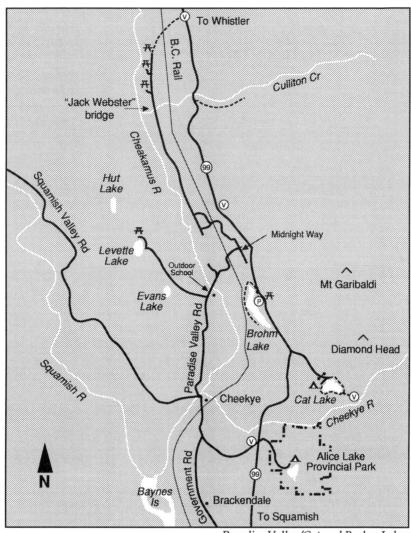

Paradise Valley/Cat and Brohm Lakes

after Highway 99 crosses the Cheekye River, look for a marker reading "Whistler—42 km," then a bridge over a small creek. Turn right onto an unmarked dirt road on the east shoulder. Almost immediately you will enter an open area with plenty of room for parking. The road from here climbs gently for 1.2 mi. (2 km). Several side roads feed off at intervals on each side. Just before the road reaches the lake, there is a small parking area and a gate. During the week you can drive right to the lakeside; on weekends, the gate bars vehicles, requiring visitors to walk in for a short distance. The steep hill beyond the gate will test both cyclists and walkers just long enough to heighten appreciation for the little lake when it swings into view.

The road divides as it reaches the lake. Stay to the right to reach the most accessible campsites. Two of the best locations for swimming or camping are on the west and north sides of the lake where there are rustic picnic tables.

Connected around the lake by a narrow trail are a half-dozen more forest campsites with far less open access to the lake. Part of the trail is actually an old logging road. A circuit of the lake on this trail is a fun-filled ride on a bicycle. A short trail at the eastern end of the lake leads to a promontory high above the Cheekye River. From here you look across towards Alice Lake. Elsewhere on the lake there are good views of the Tantalus Range rising above the treetops to the west. The open bowl of sky above the lake fills with stars in the evening. Not every night is party-time on Cat Lake; on quieter nights it can be quite pleasant. Just don't walk around in the dark without your shoes on.

BROHM LAKE   If you like Cat Lake, you'll love Brohm. It boasts easier access and many more rope swings, and is much better maintained. And what a deceptive lake—it appears to be only a diminutive, reed-filled pond until you park and walk around the corner of the ridge that shields most of it from view.

Until Highway 99 was widened and improved in 1990, there was only a small approach at the lake's south end. Fishermen still use this pull-off. Now there is a large parking lot with a walk-in launching spot for small boats and rafts closer to midlake. As summer proceeds tall reeds grow up out of the water at the south end of the lake, making it difficult to penetrate to the open water beyond. Still, it's fun to hear the swish of the hollow stalks on the hull of a canoe.

An interconnected series of trails along the east side of the lake, at water level and on the ridge above, leads past a number of rough campsites. Most of the lake is surrounded by steep rock cliffs, but there are level spots at its north end where the water is also somewhat shallower. The trails around Brohm are more difficult to negotiate than the level one around Cat. Trying to take a bike on them is more trouble than it's worth.

There is no real beach on Brohm Lake, only a gravelled area by the boat launch. The shoreline drops away sharply on all sides; keep an eye on small children. To find the best swimming spots, walk north beside the lake from the parking lot. They begin to appear almost immediately. Ropes hang from the substantial branches of several old-growth cedars that have anchored themselves to the ridge. The rock walls of the basin that holds the lake create a great echo effect, amplifying the shrieks of rope-swingers several times over. They do the same for heavy-metal

Freshwater fun at Brohm Lake.

music played late at night. If you like to howl rather than sleep, this is the campsite for you.

Just north of Cat Lake, Brohm Lake has the advantage of being situated beside Highway 99. You can arrange to be dropped off or picked up by Maverick Coach (662-8051 in Vancouver, 898-3914 in Squamish, 932-5031 in Whistler, and 894-6818 in Pemberton). This appeals to young campers, who can organize their first independent camping trip without having to ask for the family car.

WHISTLER |

WHISTLER PIONEERS

The Whistler Valley was wild and secluded for millennia. Originally, only the moccasin-clad feet of Indian traders traversed the 75 mi. (120 km) between the small settlements on the Squamish River and the shores of Lillooet Lake. The Pemberton Trail, as the early European explorers named it, ran from the top of Howe Sound through the Coast Mountains to the Pemberton Valley, linking the native peoples of Squamish and Mount Currie. Alta Lake, where Whistler now stands, was traditionally a neutral zone.

In the late 1850s two employees of the Hudson's Bay Company, seeking new trade routes to the interior, were the first Europeans to see the trail. As they travelled through the Whistler Valley they named the largest of the group of lakes they found there Summit Lake (later renamed Alta Lake) and the mountain that towered above it London Mountain (now Whistler Mountain). In 1873, the Canadian Pacific Railway sponsored the cutting of a horse trail from Howe Sound to Pemberton. The B.C. Department of Public Works upgraded the trail from Squamish to Lillooet until 1878, hoping it would serve as a cattle trail to supply settlers in Moodyville (near present-day Vancouver).

Accounts by early Pemberton ranchers of cattle drives through the Whistler Valley on this trail are filled with horrendous incidents. Both men and beasts had to be nimble on their feet, a skill still required when you walk beside the Green River towards Nairn Falls near Pemberton, or in the Cheakamus Canyon—imagine how difficult it must have been to cross any of the major rivers on foot with a reluctant Bossy in tow.

Outdoor recreation was growing in popularity with city dwellers when Vancouver restaurateurs Alex and Myrtle Philip were guided to Alta Lake in 1912 by one of their customers, John Millar (who spelt his name with an *e* after he moved to Pemberton.) They came to fish for rainbow trout. Millar, a native Texan, had built a cabin on the Pemberton Trail, outfitting it with a solid mahogany table. The muskrat stew and huckleberry pie he served earned him the nickname "Mahogany" among travellers who spent the night at his cabin. Not because his cooking tasted anything like wood—far from it—but because his patented call when dinner was served was, "Time to put your feet under the mahogany."

The party of three took the ferry *Bowena* from Vancouver's Coal Harbour to Newport (now Squamish), then hired a buckboard to get them as far as the Bracken Arms Roadhouse in Brackendale. From there they took packhorses to a small roadhouse near Alice Lake, where they prepared to climb along the Pemberton Trail through the Cheakamus Canyon to Bear Mountain, the most challenging part of the trip. They reached Millar's cabin just south of Alpha Lake the following afternoon.

The smell of fresh bread from Millar's oven in the clear morning air, coupled with the sight of schools of rainbow trout in the nearby lakes, was enough to hook the Philips on the idea of living at Alta Lake. In 1914 they bought 10 acres (4 ha) of land on the northwest corner of the lake for $700. Myrtle, her brother Phil Tapley, and her father built Rainbow Lodge that summer. It was completed just in time for the arrival of the Pacific Great Eastern Railway that fall. (Phil later settled a parcel of land at the north end of Alta Lake, still referred to as Tapley's Farm, that his father had purchased in 1925.)

In the spring of 1915 the Pacific Great Eastern Railway approached the Philips with a plan: for $2.50 per round-trip they would bring passengers to the new lodge where guests could stay for $2 a week, all-inclusive. The first party, consisting of 25 fishermen, arrived in April. Upon returning

---

WHISTLER MUSEUM

The Whistler Museum, located at the south end of town on Highway 99, has preserved the history of the valley in a series of exhibits. The museum is housed in a large portable building that once served as the town hall. Volunteers, led by longtime Alta Lake resident Florence Petersen, have created a warm environment in which visitors can gain an appreciation for the pioneers who contributed to Whistler's success. An entire room is devoted to a collection of Alex and Myrtle Philip's memorabilia (including Myrtle's first ski suit, purchased from an Eaton's catalogue). Another room contains photographs and equipment of those who opened up Whistler Mountain for skiing and who brought glory to the town through their competitive accomplishments. A slide show is available for groups interested in wildlife of the Whistler Valley. The museum is open on weekends during the winter, and from Wednesday to Sunday during summer months. Hours are 10 AM to 4 PM. Call 932-2019 for more information.

to Vancouver they spread the news about Rainbow Lodge. Soon, it was Myrtle who assumed the mantle of fame for her cooking.

Myrtle and Alex had timed their move to Alta Lake perfectly. Rainbow Lodge expanded from the original four bedrooms and a dormitory until it could accommodate a hundred guests in the lodge and nearby guest cottages. By the 1940s it was the most popular camping lodge west of Jasper.

After 33 years in business, the Philips sold Rainbow Lodge to Alec and Audrey Greenwood in 1948, against Myrtle's better judgement. She felt lost without it. As well as being the first lady of Alta Lake she had also served as postmistress for more than 30 years, operating from the small general store at the lodge. She saw everyone as they came to collect their mail, hearing their opinions and sharing their news. Although she and Alex had no children of their own, Myrtle maintained an active interest in the education of all the children of Whistler until she was in her nineties. The town's elementary school is named in her honour. After Alex's death in 1968 at the age of 86, Myrtle stayed on at Alta Lake in a small cabin on the lake's west side. She outlived Rainbow Lodge, which was lost in a fire in 1977. Myrtle died in 1986 at the age of 95; she and her sister Jean Tapley are buried beside each other in the Whistler Cemetery. The memory of the Philips and Rainbow Lodge is preserved in a park located at the original site on Alta Lake.

The Philips witnessed many changes in the Whistler Valley during this century. In 1965, when Alex was invited to throw the B.C. Hydro switch that brought electricity to the valley, it was almost symbolic of

---

WHISTLER TRANSIT

The Whistler Transit System operates daily, from 5:45 AM until past midnight. It serves neighbourhoods along Highway 99 from Tamarisk to Emerald Estates. At present the fare is $1.25 (exact change) unless you are just travelling within Whistler Village, which is a fare-free zone. Buses make round-trips every 15 or 30 minutes (depending on the time of day) on three routes: the Village Loop, Whistler Creek, and Alpine-Emerald. Some Whistler Creek runs go as far south as Function Junction. There are 12 stops at key locations throughout the valley. Ski racks are located on the outside of buses; poles and snowboards must be carried inside. Call 932-1BUS for a detailed schedule. Maverick Coach Lines makes two stops in Whistler, on Village Gate Drive and at Nesters Mall (where the freight office is also located). Maverick serves Whistler from Vancouver, Squamish and Pemberton. (In Vancouver phone 662-8051; in Whistler, 932-5031.)

the larger changes to come. You could still choose to light your lamps with kerosene, but now there were other options too. Travel patterns in the 1960s saw fewer people staying at Whistler for weeks at a time. The era of the old lodges began to end as roads improved; visitors could drive up for the day. No longer isolated, Whistler was now Vancouver's backyard playground. Even though many winter visitors had skied around Whistler, Myrtle Philip thought the sport was too expensive to gain widespread popularity. But an increase in the standard of living encouraged more people to ski, heralding the rise of Whistler as the winter destination we know today.

In 1960, the Garibaldi Olympic Development Association (GODA) was formed by members of the Canadian Olympic Committee, led by Dave Mathews of Vancouver and Sidney Dawes of Montreal, who had attended the 1960 Winter Olympics in Squaw Valley. They felt that Canada had the potential to host future games and began to survey possible sites in the Vancouver area. After an extensive survey of the Lower Mainland from Manning Park to Diamond Head, they focussed on Whistler Mountain in Garibaldi Provincial Park. (They weren't the first ones to be interested in Whistler Mountain. Stefan Ples had moved to Alta Lake in 1959 from Austria and started the Tyrol Ski Club. Club members regularly hiked up Whistler Creek to ski on the Whistler Glacier.)

With the encouragement of GODA, Franz Wilhelmsen, originally from Norway and for whom the long Franz run on Whistler Mountain is named, formed the Garibaldi Lift Company in 1962. The objectives of the GLC were to carry out feasibility studies and then build and operate lifts—this at a time when there was no road within 30 mi. (50 km) of the mountain, no electricity, no water supply and no immediate source of funding. The GLC hired Austrian Willy Schaeffler from the Fédération Internationale du Ski (the governing body of competitive skiing), who had designed the race courses for the 1960 Squaw Valley Winter Olympics. Accompanied by Wilhelmsen and Ples, he hiked Whistler repeatedly in the early '60s, checking snow conditions and amassing data on which to plan trails.

The original development plan called for three lifts running up the north face of Whistler from the present town centre. As there was a series of mining claims already staked on that face and up Fitzsimmons Creek, the B.C. government insisted the GLC use the west side. This actually worked to the GLC's advantage as only two lifts were required to reach the top, which left extra funds for two T-bars on the glacier.

The B.C. government was persuaded to build a connector road from Brackendale to Alta Lake by an alliance of valley residents and the GLC. A rough-hewn extension of the old hydro service road reached Whistler Mountain by 1964. At that time it took upwards of 5 hours to make the

45-mi. (72-km) drive. By the time Whistler officially opened for business on February 15, 1966, the road had been paved.

When John Millar first walked into Alex and Myrtle Philip's restaurant over 80 years ago, he set many changes in motion. Whistler's transition from wilderness to playground has been rapid, and not without growing pains, but the wild beauty that drew the Philips is still here for us to enjoy. As you walk the trails and climb the mountains, take a moment to thank the three who championed this land.

6 | BLACK TUSK AND GARIBALDI LAKE

CAMPING ◄
FISHING ◄
HIKING ◄
PADDLING ◄
PICNICKING ◄
SWIMMING ◄
VIEWPOINTS ◄
X-C SKIING ◄

This is really two destinations in one. In fact, the trail to Garibaldi Lake and the Black Tusk offers so many choices for adventure that you could easily revisit the area for years before exhausting the possibilities.

Black Tusk is the magnet that has been attracting attention since the first mountaineers arrived to explore it in 1912. No other rock formation in the surrounding fortress of Coast Mountain peaks is as noticeable or so readily identifiable as the Black Tusk. We know that the pillar of volcanic rock we see today is the remnant of a much larger lava flow that vented on these slopes, but its formation is still not well understood. Geologists are almost certain that it predates the zenith of the most recent ice age, which ended 12,000 years ago.

Before the coming of the Europeans, the Black Tusk was known as the "landing place of the Thunderbird" to the Squamish people. They believed that the magic Thunderbird lived on the top of the Black Tusk, flapping its wings to cause thunder and shooting lightning bolts from its eyes at anyone who came too close. They observed a taboo against climbing any of the mountains.

Visiting the Black Tusk-Garibaldi Lake region is a living lesson in geological history. With a little effort you can learn to read the story written in the rock over which you travel and the glaciers that fill the mountainscape. To begin, though, let your imagination be stimulated and your curiosity aroused by a casual, recreational visit to the site.

THE BARRIER   The turnoff to Black Tusk and Garibaldi Lake is just south of Daisy Lake, 12 mi. (19 km) from Whistler. Watch for the B.C. Parks signs on Highway 99. This paved road runs 1.6 mi. (2.5 km) east to a large parking lot beside Rubble Creek. A 5.6-mi. (9-km) trail to Garibaldi Lake begins here. There are campgrounds beside the lake and in nearby Taylor Meadows, 4.7 mi. (7.5 km) from the parking area.

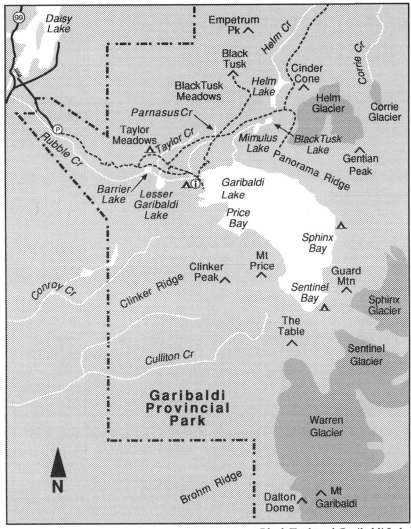

Black Tusk and Garibaldi Lake

Along the way the elevation gain is 2673 ft. (810 m) to the lake, and slightly more to the meadows.

Due to the instability of the Barrier, the rock wall rising above Rubble Creek, there is a ban on overnight camping in a wide area below the parking lot. This ban accounts for the numerous signs posted along the highway between the canyon and Daisy Lake, warning motorists not to stop. The Barrier's most recent slide occurred in 1855, blocking the flow of the Cheakamus River and creating Daisy Lake. Water levels in the lake rose even higher after B.C. Hydro dammed it in 1964.

The aptly named Black Tusk.

Even if you don't intend to walk the trail you should at least drive the short distance in from Highway 99 to the parking lot to enjoy the wide-open view of the Barrier. It stands as a broad wall of red volcanic rock, especially appealing when lit by the setting summer sun. It's a unique formation in this region, the result of a flow of molten lava coming face to face with a glacier that once occupied what is now Rubble Creek. The ice cooled and hardened the lava, forming the thick rock face that holds back the waters of Garibaldi Lake, a basin that filled as the surrounding glaciers melted and retreated.

The name Rubble Creek speaks for itself. It's not surprising to find the creek's banks lined with boulders left from the last great slide and the steadily eroding features of the Barrier. The waters of the creek are frothy white in late summer when the snowmelt is at its climax. For these reasons it's difficult to approach the creek to refresh yourself. An old overgrown trail follows the creek towards the apron of talus rock at the foot of the Barrier.

You can walk from the parking lot to the "4 km" sign in an hour along an easy trail that starts straight and then changes to switchbacks farther up the mountain. The Douglas firs and red cedars lining the beginning of the trail are smaller in girth than those higher up, a result of the great landslide that wiped out much of the forest at lower levels. Only trees that weren't in the slide path predate 1855. The ones lower down have all taken root in the years since then.

You will be relieved to reach the "6 km" marker because by now you may be suffering from visual deprivation. There are no views from the trail until just past this important divide. At the small shelter is a map of the area to help you decide which way to head from this point. The trail to the left leads up to Taylor and Black Tusk meadows and beyond there to the Tusk itself, as well as a host of other destinations. The trail to the right leads almost immediately to the viewpoint for which you've been waiting. Take a few minutes to enjoy the view even if you are not intending to follow the trail beyond to Garibaldi Lake, 1.9 mi. (3 km) farther along. A large family of chipmunks will be happy to see you as you emerge from the forest onto the open rock face. They are used to visitors and will happily leap into your lap to accept a snack as you sit enjoying the splendid vista. Next to you is the Barrier. Its face is shaded in the morning light, a subdued texture compared to its visage later in the day. To the southwest you can see from the broad white swath of the Tantalus Range rising above the Squamish Valley and around to Powder Mountain above the Callaghan Valley.

GARIBALDI LAKE   Depending on what time of year you visit, water may or may not be flowing out of nearby Barrier Lake. The outflow occurs only in late summer when water levels are at their highest. Year-round the waters from Barrier, Lesser Garibaldi and Garibaldi lakes percolate down through a layer of scoria (porous volcanic rock), venting into Rubble Creek through a series of springs at the base of the Barrier. This explains how water levels in the creek can be so high beside the parking lot despite the modest proportions of the outflow feeding it from the lakes. Bottom drainage also accounts for low water levels in the three lakes in late spring and early summer.

The best time to enjoy the visual delight of the three lakes is in August; not only are water levels at their highest but this is also when they are

After a few hours on the trail, hikers pause at the mouth of Garibaldi Lake to enjoy the view.

the most intense blue. The colour is a result of very fine sedimentation in the water, so fine that its reflection approaches the wavelength of visible light. Earlier in the summer the particles washing into the lakes from winter snowmelt are larger, resulting in cloudier hues.

Just around the corner from the viewpoint the scene is even more astonishingly beautiful. Barrier Lake lies spread like a table before you. Fish jump in full profile. Without turning your head you can see whitewater entering and leaving the small lake at each end. If you look back along the trail you'll see Cloudburst Mountain framed by the notch at the lake's west end. You'll have a bounce in your step as you walk around Barrier Lake to Lesser Garibaldi Lake because it feels so good to be here. Near the bridge over Taylor Creek, whose waters feed into Lesser Garibaldi Lake, there is an approach to the lakeside that fishermen will find helpful. The trail rings the lake on the hillside above but offers little other access.

Past the lake the trail enters the forest once more, dividing again just before the "8 km" sign. The trail to the left is one of several leading to the Taylor Meadows campground. You are now cloistered among the evergreens, 15 minutes from Garibaldi Lake. This is to prepare you for the screamingly grand views that await at the big lake. From the bridge over Parnasus Creek you may see other hikers taking in the view from a bridge over the outflow creek from Garibaldi Lake, framed in a notch of red volcanic rock and evergreens with the white of the glaciers behind them. By this time you may be wondering whether your nervous system can handle the volume of visual stimuli being fed to your brain.

Cross the bridge and walk (or wade) around to the Garibaldi Lake campground. There are three dozen campsites scattered on the hillside above the lake. Some of them have wooden platforms on which to pitch a tent, helpful when the ground is wet. You are allowed a stay of up to 14 days. At present the fee per night is $6. There are four covered shelters for day use, with picnic tables situated both inside and in front of them. Nearby, the team of rangers that patrol the park and put on interpretive programs for visitors have a cabin of their own.

Just offshore are the Battleship Islands, a string of small, rocky outcroppings. Several are lightly forested. You can walk out to them when water levels are low enough; otherwise you'll have to wade or swim. Water temperatures in the big lake are rarely high enough to be enjoyable, but if the sun is shining it will help warm you up once you emerge. There are several benches along the lakeside trail and on the largest island. A sign on the lakeside trail lets you know that you've reached the "9 km, Elev. 1470 m" mark. For kids who have made the journey this is a good place to let them loose. When lake levels are at their highest, sections of the boardwalk leading out to the islands double as rafts from which kids can swim, fish or just stretch out and relax.

Getting here is easy enough. The challenge is deciding where to head next. Before doing anything else it's a treat to sit looking out at the surroundings, trying to put a name to the many peaks and icefields. The trail around the lake runs only a short distance past the campground. You'll meet the occasional visitor carrying paddles and an inflatable boat—one way to visit parts of Garibaldi Lake that would otherwise take some serious hiking to reach. There are wilderness camp shelters at several locations near the south end of the lake.

BLACK TUSK   For many people the most obvious direction to head from Garibaldi Lake or Taylor Meadows is toward the Black Tusk, even

Climbing the meadow trail towards the Black Tusk.

if they don't plan to climb to the top. A trail from Garibaldi Lake climbs through the forest above the lake, meeting up with the trail from Taylor Meadows after a 30-minute walk. Along the way it passes a series of small ponds sprinkled on the mountainside. The views from the open meadows around these ponds change constantly as you gain altitude. Very few peaks emerge from the Sphinx Glacier predominent in the east. It's a vast névé, a permanent icefield. Not all glaciers are in retreat—at higher elevations they may be growing even larger as unmelted snow accumulates from year to year. Over time, as old snow is covered by new, the compression creates glacier ice.

Below you Garibaldi Lake unfolds, revealing the full extent of its long contour. It is so large that parts of its surface lie undisturbed while others are patterned by the play of the wind. The meadows are more spacious up here than in almost any other part of Garibaldi park, with the possible exception of the Diamond Head Trail. A set of parallel trails climbs towards the Black Tusk Meadows; 50 years ago, packhorses bringing supplies to large camps in the meadows wore these deep ruts, which have eroded further with each spring's run-off. Restoration work continues to repair the delicate tundra.

Squadrons of small butterflies accompany you as you make your way to the trailhead marker in the Black Tusk Meadows, where you will also find an interpretive sign and an outhouse. Climbers already on top of the Tusk look like clusters of insects from here. At this point there is a choice of several trails: you may climb to the Black Tusk, 1.9 mi. (3 km) above, or head to Helm Lake and Panorama Ridge, closer by. The Helm trail leads north to Cheakamus Lake, 8.7 mi. (14 km) distant, through a distinctly volcanic zone. Even if you are not prepared to go the distance, you can still visit the area a little over a mile away around the lake and glacier. From Panorama Ridge, 1.9 mi. (3 km) farther along, you get unlimited views around Garibaldi Lake, with features that are hidden at lower altitudes now revealed in detail. To the south, the peaks of Mount Garibaldi rise higher than all others.

The trail to the Tusk begins to climb steadily towards a nearby ridge (the trick is to take baby steps much of the way). Little streams constantly parallel or cross the trail. Take along a small cup with which to refresh yourself. Even if you find the hike strenuous, it's worth going at least a short distance up the trail to get a view of Garibaldi Lake. The meadows on all sides are blooming with blue lupine, red heather, Indian paintbrush, and yellow cinquefoil.

If you persist, in an hour you will reach the ridge. Now nothing stands in the way of views of the Black Tusk's south face. At this point the last of the alpine firs fade away and a barren expanse of degenerating granite takes over. A dusty trail leads across the flats and up to the Tusk, whose peak is still another hour away. On top you can see every place from which you've ever viewed the Tusk, and then some.

You'll have to psyche yourself up to accomplish the last stage of the journey to the top. The going isn't easy, and it's not for novices; it helps to be 18 or at least in the company of youthful energy. Otherwise you may be content to drink in the views from the shelter of a nearby grove while you picnic. You can now see Mimulus and Black Tusk lakes below. The trails to Helm and Panorama Ridge pass beside them. Even at this altitude you'll find hummingbirds keeping you company. If you have a brightly coloured piece of clothing with you, spread it on the ground and sit quietly nearby. A hummer will soon be along to check out this strange flower.

TAYLOR MEADOWS   As you walk through Taylor Meadows the Black Tusk towers above while Garibaldi Lake is hidden from view. The western skyline predominates in this open area. A network of board-walks leads through the campsites in the meadow, helping protect the delicate alpine soil from the many pairs of feet that walk through here each year. The old log cabin in the meadow, now used to house park equipment, once quartered a crew of hydrologists dispatched by Major Taylor in the 1930s to investigate the energy-generating potential of the region. There is a covered cooking shelter nearby.

An amazing number of visitors are attracted to the Black Tusk and Garibaldi Lake. If you can arrange to go on a weekday you will have it more to yourself. On weekends, the trail back to the parking lot at the end of the day can be as congested as the highway—just be patient and revel in your new memories.

DAISY LAKE   When the road from Vancouver to Whistler was first opened in 1965, it took a different route around the south end of Daisy Lake. You can see the old road on the left almost as soon as you make the turn from Highway 99 onto the Black Tusk-Garibaldi Lake road. If you follow the old road you will pass the south end of the dam traffic used to cross. This road runs for several miles along the east side of Daisy Lake, yielding views that you won't otherwise see. Several of the largest trees in the valley stand beside the road above the lake.

LAKE LUCILLE   Almost directly across Highway 99 from the Black Tusk-Garibaldi Lake turnoff is a crossing in the opposite direction leading to the former settlement of Garibaldi. In 1980 the last remaining residents were relocated farther up the road to Pine Ridge Estates, following a decision by the provincial government that potential land-slides posed too high a threat. There are two lovely little lakes, Lucille and Freeman, to explore nearby. Cross the B.C. Rail tracks and continue straight ahead. Watch for a trail leading west off the road. It is blocked by several large boulders. Follow this trail and you will discover Lake Lucille on the other side of a small ridge. There is a small dock at lakeside. The road climbs above Lake Lucille to Freeman Lake, a short distance beyond.

7 | BRANDYWINE FALLS

CAMPING ◄
CYCLING ◄
HIKING ◄
PICNICKING ◄
SWIMMING ◄
VIEWPOINTS ◄
WALKING ◄

There are two historic routes in the Whistler region: the Gold Rush Trail from Harrison Lake to D'Arcy, and the Pemberton Trail from Squamish to Pemberton. In a frontier land with little evidence of a past (beyond the rare traces left by pictograph painters in the Lillooet Lake region), these are important souvenirs. To walk these trails in the footsteps of those who've gone before is to see the land as they did.

When the first Europeans arrived they were welcomed by the Indians to whom the Coast Mountains have been home for thousands of years. The ancient trading route linking the peoples of the coast with those in the mountain valleys came to be known by the newcomers as the Pemberton Trail. The sense of wonder they must have felt when they walked it can still be shared today. As soon as you begin walking the old route a feeling of exhilaration wells up inside you. It's unfortunate that there are so few traces left to enjoy. A neglected trail soon becomes overgrown; all it takes is the passing of a generation for the old to be forgotten.

A section of the trail between McGuire and Brandywine Falls is still there for the crossing. As you walk along you have time let your imagination conjure up the faces of those who walked here before you. You can easily make the journey in a day, beginning from the provincial park at Brandywine Falls or from the Cal-Cheak Forest Service Recreation Site near McGuire.

BRANDYWINE FALLS PROVINCIAL PARK   If you don't have the time or the energy to approach Brandywine Falls from afar, you can drive to within a few minutes' walk of the observation platform beside it. Nearby is a provincial park with 15 camping spots and a day-use picnic area. There is a charge for overnight use from May to October. Bounded by Highway 99 and the B.C. Rail line, this is an extremely popular park on summer weekends.

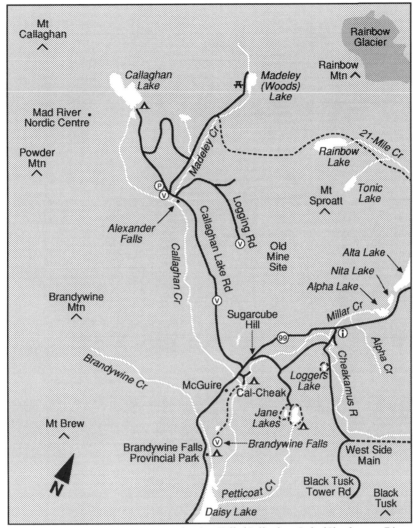

Brandywine Falls/Callaghan Lake/Cheakamus River

Walking to the falls from the park will take 10 minutes. The well-marked trail begins from the parking lot. Cross a bridge over Brandywine Creek, then go a short distance farther on the railway tracks, and you'll soon be there. A short path leads through the woods beside the creek until just before the water spills over the rim into the canyon below. The creek may look benign, but don't be fooled—that's a strong current. Children should be discouraged from playing on the smooth banks as there are very few handholds along the edge.

Spray from the water spilling out into the carved gorge 218 ft. (66 m)

In winter the roar of Brandywine Falls sounds like a jet taking off.

below nourishes the lush growth on the canyon walls in summer and coats it with an icy glaze in winter. Nearby Daisy Lake takes in the waters from the creek and elsewhere, but it lies far below the observation platform at the waterfall. It's evident that over time the creek has worn away the rock considerably.

The falls take their name from a bit of surveyor's lore about the deep pool directly beneath the falls. It's said that many bottles of brandy and wine were wagered in a contest to guess the falls' actual height, and the empty bottles were supposed to have been at the bottom of the pool. Divers explored it several years ago, but found nothing for their efforts.

CAL-CHEAK FOREST SERVICE RECREATION SITE If you choose the longer route to Brandywine Falls, you can walk part of the Pemberton Trail. This route also takes you to the Cal-Cheak recreation site, such an interesting location that it can be a destination in itself. Cal-Cheak takes its name from the two bodies of water that converge here, Callaghan Creek and the Cheakamus River. There are actually three sites in one at Cal-Cheak: a day-use picnic area on the banks of Callaghan Creek, camp spots at the north site on the Cheakamus River, and another camping area at the south site where the waterways meet. The forest around the picnic area and the south site is particularly imposing.

Traffic speeds along Highway 99 north of Brandywine Park as the road nears Whistler. Don't let the pressure of keeping up with the pack make you miss the turn to Cal-Cheak. There are no signs on the roadside to indicate that you're approaching it. You'll have to keep your eyes peeled to see the modest brown sign beside the railway tracks where a dirt road crosses going east, 2.7 mi. (4.3 km) north of Brandywine Falls Provincial Park. Coming from Whistler, it's the first road on the left south of Callaghan Lake Road.

Good picnic spots are always a welcome find. The one at Cal-Cheak is hidden from view just around the first corner of the road. There are five sturdy tables, several with barbecues, located here. One of them is covered by an A-frame shelter, especially helpful in wet weather. Another is located on the banks of Callaghan Creek on a former helicopter pad. There is an outhouse but no drinking water. If you use water from the creek or river, boil it first for 10 minutes.

There are also good picnic spots at the other two campsites. To find them, continue down the road past the picnic area. A sign points left to the north site, right to the south site. (The logging road that runs past the recreation sites continues south for quite a distance, eventually climbing the mountainside towards Empetrum Ridge.) At the north site there's a place for children to wade in a backwater of the Cheakamus if water levels aren't too high. The road through the south site runs in a semicircle past a number of tables set back in the woods. When occupancy is high, you may have trouble at first finding the path to the suspension bridge across Callaghan Creek. Watch for the gravelled approach that runs farther back into the forest than the approaches to other campsites. A short set of stairs descends to the bridge. Just before the bridge a path runs off to the left, leading first to a covered table and then to another table on a promontory where the Callaghan and Cheakamus converge. The trail descends a staircase to a campsite and picnic table beside the river. Avoid being here overnight when water levels are rising.

In late spring and well into summer Callaghan Creek runs strong with the overflow from four lakes, catch-buckets for the melted snow. Mount Callaghan sends water down to blend with the Cheakamus

The Cal-Cheak Forest Service Recreation Site at the confluence of Callaghan Creek and the Cheakamus River.

River. The whistle stop of McGuire lies just west of here, linked to the recreation site by a suspension bridge. The bridge is well fortified and screened on both sides, so there is no fear of sacrificing small children or pets to the waters rushing below, but two persons walking across it in cadence will set it bouncing and swinging giddily. A sign posted beside the bridge points the way to Brandywine Falls, 2.5 mi. (4 km) away.

Once across the bridge, stay to the left. Recent erosion has cut back the riverbank, but with one or two exceptions the trail remains intact. Within minutes you'll reach the railway tracks. There's only one small cabin left at McGuire, looking a lot less spiffy than the railway shelter on the opposite side of the tracks. It's an important spot geographically despite all appearances, given that three bridges cross Callaghan Creek near here. Without them travel of all kinds—rail, vehicular and pedestrian—would come to a halt. Log pilings from an abandoned span can still be seen west of Highway 99 on Callaghan Creek.

The Pemberton Trail runs south of McGuire to Brandywine Falls, an easy 90 minutes on foot. A bike is useful the first third of the way but will have to be stashed or carried once you hit the rocky sections and wooden staircases. Though this is not a difficult trail, there are some parts that climb and descend; young children may find it challenging, so be prepared to carry them for part of the way.

Railway surveyors once used this route as they plotted directions early in the century. Some stretches of the path are formally lined with stones. The trail crosses the railway tracks at McGuire and then twice again as it leads to the falls. At the second point, just after the trail crosses a ridge above Swim Lake, you must follow south beside the tracks for a short distance after emerging from the woods. The well-marked trail reappears just before the railway crosses a small bridge over Brandywine Creek. Caution is always necessary when walking beside the tracks, although the B.C. Rail train engineers lay a heavy hand on the whistle during their run through the Whistler Valley, and there is very little likelihood of being taken by surprise. In the off-season the BCR passenger train sometimes pauses as its cars cross the bridge here; the conductor calls out before the bridge appears so that everyone can get over to one side for a glimpse. On foot you get a more impressive view of Brandywine Creek from the nearby observation platform beside the gorge.

SWIM LAKE   Aptly named Swim Lake is one of several small ponds that the trail passes, and the most approachable. There are several clear areas from which to enter the lake, but very little shallow water in which to stand. The degenerating granite rocks on the hillside around the lake show signs of the volcanic activity that gave the Whistler area its distinct geological character. As the structure is revealed layer on layer where Brandywine Falls has worn away a wide gorge, it is easy to imagine lava and ash pouring from the cone of Black Tusk, which is directly above to the east.

8 | CALLAGHAN LAKE ROAD

CAMPING ◀
CYCLING ◀
DRIVING ◀
FISHING ◀
HIKING ◀
PADDLING ◀
SNOWMOBILING ◀
SWIMMING ◀
VIEWPOINTS ◀
X-C SKIING ◀

The turnoff onto Callaghan Lake Road from Highway 99, 3 mi. (5 km) south of Whistler, is marked by a large red sign put up by the Mad River Nordic Centre. This company has been developing cross-country trails west of Callaghan Lake Road, to make use of the superb winter snow conditions in the Powder Mountain region nearby. At present the Callaghan Lake Road is the only access. For information call Mad River Nordic Centre in Whistler at 932-5629. In winter and early spring the road becomes quite badly rutted from 4x4s; I don't recommend driving it in a conventional vehicle before the grader has been through. If you wish to explore it on skis you might be able to hitch a ride with a snowmobile. Such a service is provided on weekends during winter months. Contact Glacier Snowmobile Adventures in Whistler (938-1241) for details.

Callaghan Lake Road climbs along the north side of a wide valley past a series of clear-cut areas for 7.4 mi. (12 km) until it arrives at the shores of Callaghan Lake. Along the way, just before the road crosses a small bridge over Madeley Creek at the 4.3 mi. (7 km) point, there is a turnoff to the left leading to Alexander Falls. A brown Forest Service stake marks the turn, and it is only a short distance to a viewpoint. (See Brandywine Falls chapter for map of this area.)

ALEXANDER FALLS There is no room to camp at Alexander Falls; it is simply a viewing area. The best time for visiting is in June when water levels are highest. Shortly after dropping over the falls, Madeley Creek blends with Callaghan Creek.

An old logging road leads off to the right just before the Madeley Creek bridge and runs back along a ridge for several miles towards the old Northair mine site. Although this road is narrow and somewhat overgrown by alder, it is easy to negotiate your way to more open ground. There is a small secondary creek below the ridge for water, and

Alexander Falls, near Callaghan Lake.

plenty of space for rough camping. While others jostle for room at nearby Brandywine Park, you can be quite comfortably settled in on this ridge with a view that tops most others in the Whistler region. One of the best times of day to be up here is near sundown, when the evening light plays over the snow domes of the three Pacific Range peaks to the west: Brandywine Mountain at the southern end (the highest at 7300 ft. [2227 m]), the aptly named Powder Mountain in the middle, and Mount Callaghan to the north. A glacier joins Powder and Callaghan. This range separates the Squamish Valley from the wide Callaghan Valley spread below Mount Callaghan.

There may well be snow on the upper part of the Callaghan Lake Road until the beginning of summer. On the west side of the road, just across the bridge above Alexander Falls, is a large cleared area especially suited to recreational vehicles for overnight stays. In winter this is a staging area for snowmobilers. There are good views from here of the top of the Pacific Range.

MADELEY LAKE ROAD   Exploring on foot or by bicyle up the Madeley Lake Road (spelled Madley on some maps) can be a lot of fun. There are many sights that you might miss if you drive. It's not unusual for this 2.5-mi. (4-km) road to be blocked by an occasional blow-down. For the first part of the way to Madeley Lake the road is overgrown on each side by alders that may scratch the paint on your vehicle—another reason to leave your car back at Alexander Falls.

If you make the journey on foot it will take you a leisurely hour to walk in from Alexander Falls. The turnoff to Madeley Lake from the Callaghan Lake Road is marked by a Forest Service sign. At the halfway point you pass the junction of a road that eventually leads back to the Callaghan Lake Road, higher up the mountain. Along the way it passes beside a small lake, one of several that dot the slopes of Mount Callaghan.

Close to this junction you can walk down through the brush to get a better look at Madeley Creek. Fat marmots sunning themselves on the rocky hillside above the road may whistle at you—their loud call always catches me off guard. As you journey along, views of the summits of both Callaghan and Rainbow mountains begin to open up. The road curves around Madeley Lake to its north end; the best access point is from the south, close to where you first see the lake.

The Whistler Off-Road Cycling Association has been gradually roughing out a trail from Madeley Lake that links up with the one from Rainbow Lake. The trail begins just south of Madeley Lake and takes a full day to complete.

CALLAGHAN LAKE   Callaghan Lake Road climbs beyond Alexander Falls. In 3 mi. (5 km) you reach a large cleared parking area on Callaghan Lake's south side. The road ends here at the Forest Service recreation site. Camping is limited near the shores of this cold, modest-sized lake, as the underbrush is thick, with little level ground. Fishing is a major attraction here, with some boating and canoeing. Rising directly above is Mount Callaghan, from whose peak the waters of the lake descend and drain into the Cheakamus River, cutting through the valley below. Cool winds blow down its slopes, even in summer.

A much smaller pond for sunbathing and swimming is within 15 minutes' walk of Callaghan. There is no clear trail to the pond, but bushwacking into it is not difficult. Use Callaghan Creek on one side and the road nearby on the other as guides. Walk south, just out of sight of each, and you'll find the pond. In contrast with the lakeshore, there isn't much underbrush here to deter you. Soft glades surround much of the pond, inviting you to stretch out. As there's often quite a crowd at Callaghan Lake, you may find that this sheltered pond provides a respite from the action.

The road to Callaghan Lake provides an excellent view of the mountains on the west side of the Whistler Valley, but perhaps the most compelling reason for travelling even partway up is the view on the return trip. To the east is the Black Tusk, which stands alone before you as you descend back into the valley. Matching the view from the summits of Whistler and Blackcomb mountains, this is one of the most panoramic vantage points from which to view this snaggletooth.

After exploring both the Squamish and Callaghan valleys, you will have a new perspective on the Whistler area. Instead of finding it remote, inaccessible, a confused jumble of names, you will have developed a mental picture of how this region links up from one peak to the next, from one valley to the other. As you drive the highway you will have the satisfaction of knowing where the side roads lead; looking west or south from Whistler or Blackcomb mountains, you'll find it much easier to identify other peaks by name.

9 | CHEAKAMUS RIVER

CAMPING ◄
CYCLING ◄
DRIVING ◄
FISHING ◄
HIKING ◄
KAYAKING ◄
PICNICKING ◄
SNOWMOBILING ◄
SWIMMING ◄
VIEWPOINTS ◄
WALKING ◄
X-C SKIING ◄

As the Cheakamus River flows northwest out of Garibaldi Provincial Park and then south towards Daisy Lake it provides many opportunities for exploring along its banks. There is a wealth of good picnic spots beside it where you can relax, either before or after visiting several small lakes nearby. As the river tumbles along there are two particularly good spots favoured by kayakers. Water levels normally remain high through August; September and October are the months when you are most likely to see paddlers on the river. Even then there are many challenging sections that only experienced river runners attempt. (For a detailed description of the river's kayaking potential, check Betty Pratt-Johnson's *Whitewater Trips*.)

Three roads lead to different sections of the river: West Side Main, the Sugarcube Hill-Jane Lakes road, and the Cal-Cheak Forest Service Recreation Site road (for information on the Cal-Cheak road, see the Brandywine Falls chapter).

WEST SIDE MAIN   This is the companion to the Cheakamus Lake Road (which is also known as East Side Main). Make the well-marked turn from Highway 99 onto Cheakamus Lake Road at the south entrance to Whistler. Follow along the graded gravel road. Stay right until you reach a wooden bridge. There is a pull-out on the other side where you can stop for a look into the gorge. After crossing the Cheakamus River the road divides again. Stay to the left. A sign points the way to Loggers Lake, slightly less than 2 mi. (3 km) past the bridge. (The road to the right goes to the landfill site, a good place to watch bears—carefully—and beyond to link up with the Jane Lakes-Sugarcube Hill road.)

As West Side Main follows the Cheakamus River towards Loggers Lake there are two turnoffs to the left. The first goes in a short distance to a water-gauging station by the river. Farther along, another goes to a kayak launching spot marked by several large containers. You can park

70

here and follow an old track a short distance farther to the edge of the river.

LOGGERS LAKE   West Side Main turns rough for a short distance as it climbs uphill. The turn to Loggers Lake is well-marked. Unless you have a 4x4 with good clearance, park off the road in the cleared section. The walk from here to the lake is an easy 10 minutes. You can choose to stay beside the lake, trying your luck at fishing from several good spots, or walk the trail that loops high above the lake for 3.7 mi. (6 km). One end of the trail begins beside the road before it reaches the lake. It is well marked. Plan on taking between 1^1/$_2$ and 2 hours to complete the round-trip. By going this way and walking clockwise around the lake, you may find the going slightly easier on the steep section above the lake's south end. The other option is to follow along the road past the first trail marker, bearing right where the road divides at the lake's south end. This leads in 5 minutes to the other end of the loop trail and its marker.

Loggers Lake lies nestled in the cone of an ancient volcano, one of the most interesting and easily accessible such sites in the Whistler region. The first entrance to the trail will get you to the lake more quickly than the road does. From lakeside the trail climbs steadily in several minutes to a viewpoint above the north end of the lake. Beside the trail is one especially big conifer standing out among the many sturdy old-growth firs clinging to the moss-covered scree. The branches of the trees here are heavily laden with trailing sphagnum moss. As the trail crests the ridge it provides good views of sections of the winding Cheakamus River below. Loggers Lake passes from sight for the next while.

You can tell this was once a volcano by the curved shape of the rim that rings the lake. As the trail climbs through the forest there are several good viewing areas near the rim that reveal unique geological formations. There are three rustic wooden benches along the trail. One has a view to the southeast of Empetrum Ridge; another one looks west towards Mount Brew and the Metal Dome; the third is among the trees beside the trail, perfectly suited for sitting quietly while watching and listening to nature.

The descent from the ridge at the lake's south end is steep and rough compared to the rest of the trail. You may wish to retrace your steps rather than attempt it, especially in wet weather. Recent blow-downs seriously obscure the trail at one point. Be careful here, especially when the footing is slippery. You'll have to cross a section of scree near the bottom of the trail; watch for the orange trail markers to appear again beside a dense stand of alder. From here an old road leads around to a trailhead marker. Stay right at this point. Loggers Lake is only a few minutes beyond. Along the way you will pass a smaller, less accessible

Loggers Lake is in the crater of an ancient volcano.

lake. Stay left on the road once it reaches Loggers Lake, and it will lead you back down to West Side Main.

RIVERSIDE TRAILS   West Side Main is in good shape for another 2 mi. (3.5 km) past Loggers Lake. One of the best access points to the upper Cheakamus River is on the left side of the road a short distance past the Loggers Lake turnoff. There is room for several cars to park here. A trail leads down to a rock shelf jutting into the river, one of the best picnic spots on the Cheakamus. Another trail, taped with orange markers, runs both ways along the riverbank. The trail leads north to the Loggers Lake turnoff past several more picnic spots, or south across a good fishing stream, meeting up with West Side Main a short distance beyond. The forest along the river is quite lush, and this trail is a short, pleasant walk.

BLACK TUSK TOWER ROAD   There are several more roads leading off West Side Main. The first one, on the right past Loggers Lake, is the Basalt Spur Road, which leads back to the landfill. Farther along, West Side Main divides at a point where it begins to climb uphill. A B.C. Hydro sign points right to the Black Tusk Tower Road, 4.3 mi. (7 km) of rough switchbacks (best suited to four-wheel-drive vehicles) ending on a ridge where a microwave tower stands. The Cheakamus Challenge, an annual race for mountain bikers, is held, in part, on the Black Tusk Tower Road. World-champion off-road cyclist Cindy Devine won her first competition on it and considers this a completely hideous road on which to take a bicycle for any reason but racing.

The road to the left deteriorates rapidly and becomes quite over-grown with alder. Several unruly creeks have rearranged it in places. This one is for cyclists and bushwackers only. It will be a better trail when it's used more frequently as a link with the Helm Creek trail.

JANE LAKES   These two small but interesting lakes are nestled on the slopes of Empetrum Ridge. They can be reached on foot, by bike, or in a 4x4 vehicle. The easiest way to find them is to follow a road that begins 2.5 mi. (4 km) south of Whistler. Watch for a very distinctive geological formation known as Sugarcube Hill. It's a disintegrating mound of basalt rock beside the B.C. Rail tracks just north of and opposite to Callaghan Lake Road. There is a turnoff from Highway 99; watch for the stop sign next to the tracks. Drive across the tracks, then turn left on a rough road past Sugarcube Hill. Lined with thick alder, this road descends for 1 mi. (1.6 km) to a bridge over the Cheakamus River. Before it gets to the bridge, the road branches off to the right, leading down to a gravel bar on the Cheakamus River. There are several camping spots here overlooking a bend in the river; above are more basalt formations. If this corner were ever to crumble, the course of the river would change drastically.

The bridge over the Cheakamus is a sturdy one. Even if you aren't heading to Jane Lakes, this is a quiet spot to sit in the sun and watch the river flow. Once across the bridge, stay left. (An overgrown road to the right runs for a long distance south beside the river.) You are now on an old logging road that begins to climb moderately towards a major divide. Stay right at this divide. (The road to the left runs down to the landfill site near Loggers Lake, following the hydro line. It's a pleasant 20-minute bike ride that you may want to take back to Whistler.) If you are cycling to Jane Lakes you can expect to ride two-thirds of the way there in 1 hour. Much of the road is uphill, but there are level sections

Basalt formations on the Cheakamus River illustrate Whistler's volcanic history.

where you can catch your breath. You may wish to walk from the point where the road crosses a small stream feeding into a pothole lake on the hillside below. The road begins to deteriorate seriously as it climbs steeply uphill past here. Even 4x4s will have to take this crossing with care. On foot it will be 1 hour from this point to the lakes. The road is open and exposed to the elements—no shelter anywhere. There are some good views west across the valley as you walk along; traffic on Highway 99 is visible, as are Mount Brew and the craggy peak of the Metal Dome.

Just before you reach the lakes the road passes beside a ridge of basalt columns, dramatic evidence of the volcanic activity that rocked the valley 10,000 years ago. Each column is so perfectly formed that you would think it had been chiselled into shape. This bleached ridge stands out against the green mountainside, making it visible from Highway 99.

Bear left at all times along the upper part of the road, and it will lead you to the larger of the two lakes. There are several campsites here. The hillside around the lake is quite steep. A path leads down to a large dock across from a small island. The forest surrounding the lake has been left undisturbed by the logging that has cleared much of the nearby hillsides. A close examination of the forest floor reveals a number of exotic botanical features, including fleshy orange fungi and delicate red fuschia look-alikes with tapered bell-shaped flowers.

A trail circles the lake. Aside from the slope beside the dock, the lakeshore is rough and rather inaccessible. From the lake's south end another trail with orange markers leads off to the smaller lake nearby. The path is soft underfoot as it winds through a lovely stand of old-growth evergreens. Below it a scree slope drops down to the eastern shore of the lake. The trail skirts the scree, leading to several very large trees at the lake's south end. When you're exploring, watch for these special microclimate areas—they return the energy that nature invests in them a thousandfold.

You'll have to pick your way down the scree at the lake's south end, but only for a short distance. The trail resumes its forest flavour at lakeside now. It makes a jog to get around a small, boggy finger of the lake. You'll have to cross through tall ferns and skunk cabbage as high as your waist, balancing on two logs that have been laid side by side to help you. If the logs are overgrown by the greenery, look for orange markers posted on the trees on either side of the bog to show you where they lie. Just past here is a small clearing at lakeside. The water is surprisingly warm in the small lake.

The trail ends nearby at a marker on a side road. Follow it a short distance to reach the main road; at this point you are just downhill from the big lake.

A suggestion for a circle route on bicycle: ride 3 mi. (5 km) south from Whistler along Highway 99. Much of the way is downhill on paved shoulders. Turn off at Sugarcube Hill, ride down to the Cheakamus River, explore the Jane Lakes road, then return to Whistler following the road to the landfill site. Watch for bears as you ride along this last section of road.

10 | CHEAKAMUS LAKE

CAMPING ◄
CYCLING ◄
FISHING ◄
HIKING ◄
PADDLING ◄
VIEWPOINTS ◄
WALKING ◄
X-C SKIING ◄

This turquoise lake, a jewel in a ring of glaciated peaks, was the first place I ever explored at Whistler without my skis. I've never forgotten the soft feeling of the forest floor on the trail that leads to Cheakamus's lakeside, or the way that branches high above in the old-growth forest lend shelter from the rain or sun. I've steered a bike along the humpty-dumpty 2-mi. (3.5-km) path several times. The trail I can handle, though there are some sections where I dismount and walk for short distances. But I've never had the jam to ride the 3.7 mi. (6 km) in from Highway 99 to where the trail begins, preferring instead to drive in on the old logging road.

CHEAKAMUS LAKE ROAD   Cheakamus Lake Road (also known as East Main) starts from Highway 99 at Whistler's south end, next to the round town sign welcoming you to the resort. It's gravelled, narrow, and mostly an uphill grunt. There are usually several riders willingly having a go at it; the reward is written on their smiling faces when they soar downhill on their way home. Along the early part of the road is a series of clearings where several local logging companies are demonstrating reforestation techniques.

Though Cheakamus Lake Road is relatively short, it still seems to take a while to reach the parking lot; you may begin to wonder if you're on the right road. As long as you make an important left turn shortly after starting up the road you will be fine. This turn is marked by a brown B.C. Parks sign: "Garibaldi Park (Cheakamus Lake Parking Lot)." A caution sign warns that the rough road is narrow; take it easy and honk on the blind corners to warn others of your presence.

At the parking lot you'll find a large map detailing the trail. The boundary of Garibaldi Provincial Park is close by; from here on logging has not affected the appearance of the surroundings. Dogs are not permitted in the park—the rangers who patrol the trail will make you

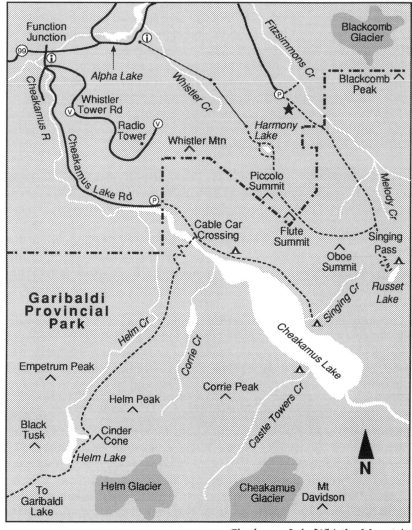

Cheakamus Lake/Whistler Mountain

turn back if you try to bring your pet with you and may also impose a $50 fine.

The trail to Cheakamus Lake does not rank as a true hike because most of the distance covered is over level terrain. Its length, however, qualifies it as an energetic walk. This is the kind of trail on which you can set your own pace. Kids can run ahead and still be heard among the tall trees. The wind blows down off the glaciated peaks, and sunbeams shatter as they try to make their way through the large branches overhead. Moss grows in a dozen shades of green on all sides of the tree trunks. Take along an extra layer of clothing to avoid getting chilled.

From the parking lot to the south end of the lake is a 1-hour walk or a 45-minute bike ride through magnificent stands of cedar, Douglas fir and western hemlock. Almost as soon as you enter the forest the rich smell of balsam greets you. The path underfoot is soft and resilient, giving each step an added bounce.

Not everyone you meet on this trail is headed for Cheakamus Lake. Some are bound for the Helm Creek trail, a major hike that begins halfway along the trail to the lake.

HELM CREEK TRAIL   Add another 30 minutes if you take the path down to the hand-hauled Helm Creek cable car. This little diversion is not a toy, but it is a lot of fun to operate, requiring the efforts of at least three adults to haul it across. The cable car connects to a trail on the opposite side of the Cheakamus River. It's a 4-hour climb from the Cheakamus River to Helm Lake, a mountain lake tucked high in the alpine. This trail eventually ties in with the Black Tusk trail. With adequate preparation you can climb the entire length in one or two days, coming out at Highway 99 south of Daisy Lake.

A very rough road leads west from Helm Creek on the opposite side of the river from the Cheakamus Lake Road. Eroded by run-off and overgrown by alder, it's in much better condition once it reaches the junction with the Black Tusk Tower Road. Check this route carefully on the map posted by the Forest Service at the start of Cheakamus Lake Road.

CHEAKAMUS LAKE TRAIL   If you choose not to take the side trip to the cable car now, continue past the Helm Creek trail intersection. The Cheakamus River will catch your ears and eyes as soon as you start on the trail. Once you enter the forest it fades from view but never from earshot. By the time you reach the Helm Creek turnoff it becomes visible again through the trees at the bottom of the steep slope. It's flowing by at a brisk rate here, especially from May through July when everywhere on the mountainside water is rushing down as if it just couldn't get away fast enough. Along the trail during these months there are many streams feeding into the lake and river. Small wooden boardwalks and bridges carry visitors across the wettest parts.

At the lake's west end the first of several clearings gives you a wide-open view out past the thick trunks of the forest. Overlord Mountain and Mount Davidson are the predominant peaks at the far east end. Directly across the lake Corrie Creek can be heard as it rushes down from little Corrie Lake hidden high up. The Cheakamus River flows quietly northwest out of the lake as it gathers momentum, then begins to raise its voice around the first corner.

Looking east to Mount Davidson from the shore of Cheakamus Lake.

There are some large logs along the shoreline from which fishermen can cast. Pan-sized rainbow trout and Dolly Varden char can be seen swimming in the clear green waters. There's more of a trick to catching them than just dangling a lure under their noses. They seem to have an ample selection of food already. As you walk the shoreline several varieties of ducks will emerge, most travelling in pairs. In spring mother mergansers appear to have their ducklings strung on an invisible tow-line behind them.

You'll see a small boat belonging to B.C. Parks tied up on the shore beside a wooden shed. It's worth the effort to portage a boat in to Cheakamus Lake, not just for fishing but also to explore unique features that you would otherwise miss. The headwaters of the Cheakamus River lie deep within Garibaldi Provincial Park. Waters from the massive icefields of the McBride Range feed the river and its tributaries as they wind their way down to the lake's east end, creating a braided, silted delta where they converge. There is a rough campsite on the shore nearby beside Castle Towers Creek.

SINGING CREEK When I originally came to Cheakamus Lake the first clearing at the west end was as far as the trail led. Since then it has gradually been lengthened along the lake's north side to reach a small camping spot 2 mi. (3.5 km) farther, beside Singing Creek. Bicycles are allowed along the entire length of the trail. I prefer to stash mine near the first blow-down, and walk the rest of the way. By the time I return to retrieve it I'm just as happy with my decision. Although many of the blow-downs from a storm several years ago have been cleared from the path, it is still a very rough ride.

As the number of visitors has increased, so has the variety of camping sites along the lake. There is even a special spot reserved for the park rangers when they are in residence. Next to it is a small creek and room for several other tents. If you plan to stay overnight at Cheakamus Lake you should take a stove, as open campfires aren't allowed in Garibaldi. The park has installed privies at two places next to the trail on the hillside above the largest campsites.

At intervals for the first 30 minutes on the Singing Creek trail you'll pass other new lakeside clearings surrounded by forest. The views seem to intensify as you move from one to the next. At one particular spot beneath a stand of healthy Douglas fir, a creek has the same high white-noise sound as a strong wind—for a moment you might imagine that the weather has taken a sudden turn for the worse.

Cheakamus Lake has moods to suit each season of the year. In winter the lake is frozen, and cross-country skiers and snowshoers get to enjoy the whiteness and the marvellous way that the boughs on the big trees hold snow. Visitors with keen eyes should look carefully on the lower trunks of trees around the first campsites. Affixed to one is a small metal sign honouring the birthplace of a baby hiker whose mother came unexpectedly to term while cross-country skiing on New Year's Day in 1983.

In spring visitors will find that the ground is damp in many places and the ground cover is just beginning to show itself. Hand-high ferns thickly carpet the slopes above the lake, providing an intensely brilliant green in the forest twilight. At several places along the way to Singing Creek, rock slides have cut paths down from the southern ridge of Whistler Mountain. As spring turns to summer, the sun warms these open scree slopes. In places the trail is so overgrown with nettles that you will want to be wearing long pants for protection. The nettles also hold the dew or raindrops; brushing past them can quickly soak a pair of jeans.

At one noticeable spot the trail crosses the hillside above the lake, where the embankment plunges steeply. This is a wildflower rock garden. It has such an orderly appearance that you might imagine someone had laboured to plant the wide variety of brightly coloured ground-hugging plants that bloom here. These small but brilliant patches of vivid orange paintbrush, wild tiger lilies, stalks of white valerian and blue lupine climb up the hillside in summer. There is a small overhang here with a shading tree, a cool spot to stop in summer to enjoy the sights of the mountainside and the lake stretched out before you. Come autumn you will no longer need its shade. With the first frosts much of the foliage begins to change hues. The quiet is uncanny in September and October as the lake awaits its first snowfall. This is a very peaceful season to visit Cheakamus.

There are no easy access points to the lake much past the rock garden on the way to Singing Creek. For the next 20 to 30 minutes the trail climbs and falls, crossing many little creekbeds, while overhead good-sized old-growth forest rears skyward. During spring run-off, or after summer rainstorms, the waters flowing down from Flute, Piccolo and Oboe summits high above on the south flank of Whistler Mountain mingle in these creekbeds, singing harmony with the wind blowing in the treetops. Added to this arrangement is the deep bass voice of Castle Towers Creek, carrying across the lake.

By the time you reach Singing Creek it will have been over 2 hours since you left the trailhead, and you will have covered more than 4 mi. (7 km). On the ridge high above you is one of the Whistler Mountain summer hiking trails. The park has plans to cut a trail linking the lake with the Singing Pass trail. For now, be content to lounge at lakeside in the hammock (cleverly woven from an old firehose) and enjoy your picnic. There is a small beach here; although the waters of Cheakamus Lake never warm up, perhaps the sun will encourage you to take a quick dip anyway.

With its splendid alpine views and the stillness of the original-growth forest, this walk will plant the seed that will bring you, your family and friends back time and again, just like the seasons.

11 | WHISTLER MOUNTAIN

CYCLING ◄
HIKING ◄
PICNICKING ◄
SKIING ◄
VIEWPOINTS ◄
WALKING ◄

Winter holds proprietary rights on Whistler Mountain for half of each year. From a skier's perspective, this is as it should be. But come the end of May the season is pretty well finished; the strengthening sun whittles away at snowbanks, revealing soggy trails and service roads that had been hidden beneath the white mantle.

Traditionally this transition time is celebrated with the Great Snow, Earth, Water Race on the slopes of Whistler Mountain and in the valley below. As many as 75 seven-member teams begin with a cross-country skier doing the first leg at the top, then handing off a baton to a teammate on downhill skis who races down the mountain until the snow runs out. Shouldering his or her equipment, the downhill skier must run the rest of the way to the bottom, where a cyclist is waiting to ride around Alta Lake. A pair of canoeists then paddle down the River of Golden Dreams to Green Lake, where the last team member waits to run with the baton around the lake and back into town to the finish line.

Early in June the last skiers to enjoy the highest slopes on Whistler are members of the National Alpine Ski Team. Whistler's Rob Boyd and his teammates gather for the first training camp leading into the next year's World Cup race season. (In March 1989, after years of victories by Canadians on the international circuit, Boyd became the first male Canadian ski racer to win a World Cup race held in Canada. Appropriately, the event was held on Whistler Mountain's challenging downhill course, rated by racers as one of the three best in the world.)

In the golden age of the lodges on Alta Lake, summer was the high season around Whistler. With the decline of the lodges, June instead marked the beginning of the quiet months following the hectic winter. But summer has come back into its own now. Many more families now visit Whistler at this time, drawn by golf courses, tennis courts, biking and walking trails, and the open waters of the lakes. When tulips and daffodils have faded back in the city, Whistler's are just beginning to blossom.

Classic Whistler Mountain.

From June to October the Whistler Mountain Express gondola ferries passengers, including those in wheelchairs or strollers, from the village to the mountaintop on a non-stop 20-minute ride with an elevation gain of 3818 ft. (1157 m). There are many options for exploring once you arrive at the top, but before you get going remember that the weather can be much cooler in the alpine than in the valley. Conditions often change quickly, so come prepared for the worst and hope for the best. If you're planning to climb into the high alpine, take sturdy, waterproof shoes and a change of socks. The going is fairly easy in the snow, but a cold dampness will set in after a while. Even in summer the air temperature on top is often a notch cooler than in the valley—a relief on a hot day, but an invitation to a bad chill if you're not prepared. The persistent breeze helps moderate body heat generated while exploring the mountain and keeps down the bugs, but pack along some repellent and a heavy sun screen (minimum SPF 15) as well as a wide-brimmed hat.

As you emerge from the Express, take a minute to enjoy the view of Whistler Mountain's peak before anything else. (See previous chapter for map of this area.) The later in the summer you go, the more of its geological makeup will be revealed by the snow melt. A rocky red apron spreads out below the peak, flanked by the browns, greys and black tones of the wide bowl. The Whistler Glacier on the north face of the mountain has shrunk over the 25 years that the mountain has been operating commercially. As a result, the Dave Murray summer ski program for children, a fixture on Whistler for many years, moved across the valley to Blackcomb's Horstman Glacier in the summer of 1991.

From the top of Whistler Mountain visitors can choose from several scenic walking or hiking routes that spread from the top of the Express in a network of well-marked roads and trails. Complimentary guided tours are available several times a day and are detailed in a brochure available at the Express ticket office. In lieu of a tour, you can choose to walk one of the easier pathways, such as the Paleface trail, for views of the valley on the Whistler Creek side of the mountain. Across to the west are the round tops of Mount Sproatt and Rainbow Mountain. The Paleface trail descends below the Roundhouse Lodge, winding its way around and under the Express in a loop that will bring you back to the lodge in 30 minutes. Along the way are many benches on which to relax while enjoying the views. By August much of the mountaintop is covered with wildflowers. Whistler Mountain's gardening staff seed many of the open slopes with grasses that turn gold as summer yields to fall. This is also the season in which low-lying berry bushes turn crimson. The colours of the rock formations and the vegetation combine to form such a pleasing picture that you can't help but slow your pace as you pass by in wonder.

Many more visitors will be inclined to climb to the open slopes above the Express. A short loop trail leads around nearby Harmony Lake which, depending on how early or late in the summer you arrive, may still be hidden under snow and ice or may already have been reduced to pond-size by its run-off into the Fitzsimmons Creek Valley far below. From Harmony Lake you can return to the Roundhouse, or descend to the Blue Chair and the service road to the village, or climb the Musical Bumps trail towards the ridge above the lake. No matter which way you turn at this point, take a minute to enjoy the view of Blackcomb Peak and the Spearhead Range to the north.

The Musical Bumps trail runs a long way east, eventually joining the

Biking on Whistler Mountain with the slopes of Blackcomb in the distance.

Singing Pass trail after 4 to 5 hours of steady climbing along the ridge. Much of the way is in Garibaldi Provincial Park, outside the region patrolled by the ski resort. For most of us the climb to the Piccolo Summit will be exercise enough. You can accomplish this in a little over 1 hour, earning a view of the entire area—literally as far as the eye can see in all directions. Black Tusk is particularly stark and dominant to the south, while Cheakamus Lake shimmers below.

Occasionally you will find a good picnic spot on a patch of bare shale. The snow all but disappears along the top of the ridge, rapidly evaporated by the wind, so the up and down of this final stretch is easy going. Hiking down through the snow is fast, and a gait not unlike skiing is possible with the right footwear.

You don't have to ride the Express in order to explore Whistler Mountain on foot. The service road leading from the village is a long but easy route to follow. The entrance is marked by a blue gate to the right of the Singing Pass access road soon after it leaves the village. Or you can simply begin beneath the Express lift and climb the slope until it meets the service road. Good views of the village and the valley open up almost immediately. It's not necessary to climb farther than mid-station to get a good workout. If you're game, you can make it to the Roundhouse in 2 hours. Total length of the road and trail from top to bottom is 5 mi. (8 km). Cyclists are not permitted on the service road unless accompanied by a certified guide.

For those who wish an escorted bike tour down Whistler Mountain, arrangements can be made at the Jim McConkey sport shop in the village. A 3-hour tour from the Roundhouse to the valley costs $39.95

Looking north at Alpha, Nita, and Alta lakes, where pioneers built the first tourist lodges.

and includes a Whistler Express lift ticket, a bike and a helmet. If you use your own bike, the price drops to $25.

WHISTLER RADIO TOWER ROAD   While the privately owned ski slopes are restricted, the rest of Whistler Mountain remains Crown land. There are several trails and roads that you can explore by bike. The Singing Pass road from the village to the boundary of Garibaldi Provincial Park is one.

Another is the Whistler Radio Tower Road. It begins from the intersection of Highway 99 and the Cheakamus Lake Road. Turn left immediately after starting up Cheakamus Lake Road. There is a large blue interpretive sign here. After a short distance on level ground the hard-packed dirt road begins to climb through alder growth; it levels out only for short distances as it gently winds and climbs toward the radio tower, 2.5 mi. (4 km) distant. Early on there is a pull-out with a good southern viewpoint.

Once you've reached the radio tower, the road continues to climb the mountainside through a series of switchbacks. This section is known as the West Ridge walking trail. Shortly past the tower it crosses a little stream flowing down from the West Bowls, in sight now high above. Take a rough spur road to the left past the creek as the main road climbs towards a switchback. At the end of this rough road is one of the most complete views of Whistler Valley. All the lakes from Alpha north to

Green lie below you. On Sunday afternoons in summer, you can watch the Laser boats racing end to end on Alta Lake from here. The views stretch all the way north to Mount Currie.

Because much of the road is hard-packed dirt, the ride back down is one of the smoothest in the valley. If you don't want to pump your bicycle to the top, organize a group with a car and driver to take the riders up. Have a look around, and then hold on for a fun descent. And don't forget to tip the driver!

12 | VALLEY TRAIL

BIRD-WATCHING ◄
BOAT RENTALS ◄
CYCLING ◄
FISHING ◄
PADDLING ◄
PICNICKING ◄
SAILING ◄
SWIMMING ◄
WALKING ◄
WINDSURFING ◄
X-C SKIING ◄

Almost entirely paved, the Valley trail passes beside seven parks, five lakes, a river and several creeks. In summer it's a cycling path and a walkway, in winter a cross-country ski trail. Whistler Village sits at its hub. The beauty of the Valley trail is that you can get on it easily from almost anywhere in Whistler. Each year it gets longer, keeping pace with the resort's growth. It's difficult to say where the trail begins and ends; most of it is a 9.3-mi. (15-km) loop.

Before you start out on the Valley trail, decide whether you are going to do the entire loop or make one of the parks or lakes your destination. On foot it will take 3 hours to walk the entire length, while by bike it will be half that or less. But you don't have to go the whole distance in order to enjoy the trail.

VILLAGE TO THE VALLEY TRAIL   Approaching from the village, you will find the Valley trail on the west side of Highway 99. Take the underpass next to the Conference Centre leading to the Whistler Golf Club, where you can link up with the main section of the trail. A large map here details the trail. Or, before you cross Highway 99, take the short section of trail that leads south past the Tantalus Lodge to the Brio neighbourhood. Cross the highway here to get to the main trail beside the 16th hole of the golf course.

The other option from the village is to join up with the Valley trail as it heads north towards Lost Lake. Cross Blackcomb Way, following the signs to the Lost Lake trailhead, just north (to the left) of the intersection of Valley Gate Boulevard and Blackcomb Way. It is well marked and there is a large parking lot beside it. A map posted here will give you a detailed look at the trail system. Just down the trail is the Whistler Skatebowl where skateboarders play.

Alternatively, on Blackcomb Way just south (to the right) of this same intersection, cross at the traffic light to get to Fitzsimmons Creek. Take

Arnold Palmer designed the Whistler Golf Club to take advantage of the spectacular mountain backdrops.

the covered wooden bridge across the creek, then stay to the left on a dirt trail beside the creek rather than heading uphill to the Blackcomb chairlift. Both the Lost Lake section of the Valley trail and the Fitzsimmons Creek trail follow the creek for a short distance north before a bridge links them. A network of cross-country ski trails around Lost Lake, suited to walking or cycling in summer, begins from this point.

LOST LAKE PARK Lost Lake used to be just that: remote, difficult to find, its warm waters a haven for skinny-dippers. In the past decade, with the development of Blackcomb Mountain, Lost Lake has become a much more sought-after destination.

Many of the trails around Lost Lake are marked with interpretive signs that will help you assess the level of difficulty of each one. These signs give a graphic illustration of the ups and downs that you will encounter along the way. The steeper the curve, the more effort you will have to put into them. These are effective not only during winter months, but also in summer when the trails are used for cycling. Not all the trails lead directly to Lost Lake—stay right at all points for the quickest approach to the beach. Centennial, Old Mill Road and Panorama are the major trails, but a warren of narrower tracks also crosshatches this area.

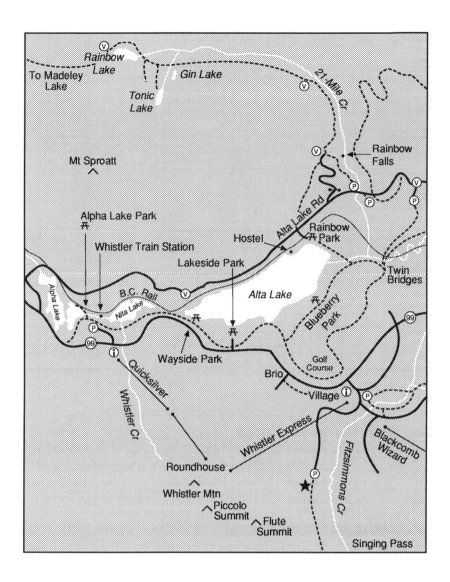

A wide road, more for winter than summer use, has taken the place of the rough trail that used to circle the lake. Walkers and cyclists would have been satisfied with a narrower path; however, innovations in the sport of cross-country skiing have brought about a widening of the trail to accommodate both track-style and skating-style skiing.

A beach has been built up on the east end of Lost Lake. Picnic tables, barbecues and a smooth lawn lend a very pleasant appearance to the park. The shallow swimming area here is more enjoyable for junior swimmers than the steep drop-offs at other points around the lake. For

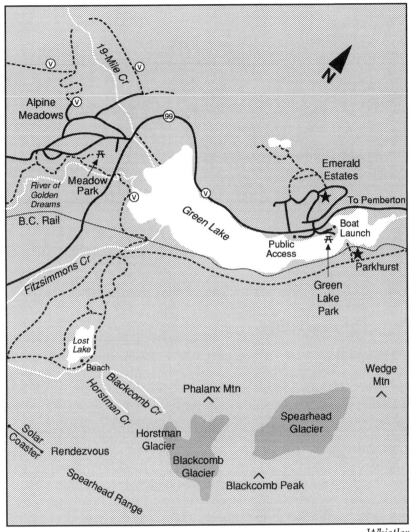

Whistler

those who like to sun on a dock, try the one on the north side of the lake. There are still semi-private locations at the west end of the lake from which you can swim even if you have forgotten your bathing suit.

THE LOOP TRAIL   Beginning from the golf course you have a choice of two directions in which to head. The Loop section of the Valley trail runs past the village. Following it clockwise, head north past the Whistler Golf Club, along the River of Golden Dreams to Meadow Park, across Highway 99 to Green Lake, then turn south to Lost Lake and back into

People-watching is always great in Whistler Village, especially on warm summer days.

the village. It is 6.3 mi. (10 km) long; it takes 90 minutes to walk and is mostly level except for the section around the Lost Lake. Before crossing the River of Golden Dreams on the north side of the Whistler Golf Club, the Valley trail sends out an arm leading to Rainbow Park on Alta Lake's northwest corner. This section takes 15 minutes to walk one-way.

RAINBOW PARK   It's fitting that one of the prettiest locations on Alta Lake should be the site of a large park, doubly so since Rainbow Park is the location of the original lodge that first attracted recreational visitors to the valley. Rainbow Lodge stood here from 1915 to 1977 when it was destroyed by fire. Ten years later the municipality began clearing the shoreline for a park. It is now a popular place for windsurfers to launch; a section of the beach is reserved exclusively for them and for boaters. A large dock floats offshore for swimmers. A number of old log cabins have been brought to the park from other locations on the lake. These are gradually being restored. You can take the Valley trail here, or you can drive to the entrance of the park via Alta Lake Road.

Immediately after the Valley trail crosses the railway tracks past the turnoff to Rainbow Park, a rough trail leads off to the west. It climbs past an old gravel pit, through the wildlife refuge, and connects with Alta Lake Road. The 2.5-mi. (4-km) section of the Valley trail that runs from the railway tracks to Meadow Park is the longest stretch of level pavement in the entire trail network. It passes close beside the River of

Rainbow Park is the site of the valley's first tourist whistle stop.

Golden Dreams at several points. Yellow skunk cabbages sprout beside the trail in many places. Their unmistakable odour is prevalent in spring, and in later months the size of the green leaves on these plants is astounding.

MEADOW PARK   Of all the parks in the valley, Meadow Park is the largest. In addition to the six picnic tables with barbecues set up on the banks of the River of Golden Dreams, there is an extensive system of playing fields and tennis courts, plus an imaginatively designed children's play area. To drive to the park rather than take the Valley trail, take the entrance off Rainbow Drive in the Alpine Meadows neighbourhood. Watch for the signs pointing to the park at the intersection of Camino and Rainbow.

MEADOW PARK TO LOST LAKE   North of Meadow Park the Valley trail follows the River of Golden Dreams to the south side of Green Lake. From here you have some of the best views on the whole trail. In the cool hours of early morning and again towards sundown, mist rises from the surface of the River of Golden Dreams as it enters the lake. A narrow side trail to the west of the Valley trail leads along the banks of the river as it flows around its last few bends. Watch for the rough trail leading off to the west of the Valley trail. It forms a loop, with one entrance next to the log footbridge spanning the river, the other marked by a tall brown stake close to the shore of Green Lake. This loop trail has been upgraded by

The Valley trail along Green Lake offers this view of Mount Weart.

members of the Whistler Off-Road Cycling Association, who have laid down gravel on some of the muddier sections and placed orange trail markers to help guide your way. Tall Sitka spruce, black cottonwood and poplar trees line the riverbank. Bird-watching is good here. Much of the trail is overgrown by tall grass and berry bushes during summer months; wear long pants, but prepare to get wet even then after a rain or at times of heavy dew. You may surprise an occasional beaver working the river near sundown, causing it to slap its tail in warning. The trail is wild in places, and you'll find flowers blooming in many shades during summer. Particularly striking are groups of strawberry-coloured Indian paintbrush amid tall stalks of white yarrow. Each section of the trail provides its own views. If you walk upstream from Green Lake you will come to a spot where the glacier on the north face of Whistler Mountain beams across the valley at you. Its wide-open stretch of sculpted whiteness reminds you of how hidden the glaciers on Blackcomb Mountain are by comparison.

There is a bench beside the Valley trail on Green Lake. From here you can watch the peaks on the east side of the valley reflect in tableau on the still surface of the water at dawn and sunset. Wedge Mountain is unmistakable. Beyond it is Mount Weart, with the volcanic ridge named the Owls fanned out behind it. Mount Moe and the Hibachi Ridge lead up to the solid mass of Mount Currie.

The Valley trail runs along the open shore of Green Lake past the summer seaplane base and then enters a long lane lined with alder. It crosses the railway tracks and heads uphill to a bridge over Fitzsimmons Creek. A short distance above here, a trailmarker directs you back into the forest past the hydro lines. (See the Green Lake Hydro Trail to Parkhurst chapter for a description of the trail leading up the east side of Green Lake.) From this point you have your choice of a variety of trails leading around Lost Lake. Keep left at any junction if your immediate destination is Lost Lake, a 15-minute walk away. Past Lost Lake, the Valley trail loops back to Whistler Village.

ALTA LAKE   South of the trail map at the Whistler Golf Club, the Valley trail borders the golf course to the Blueberry Hill neighbourhood. This section is treed—good protection against wayward golf balls. Rainbow Mountain can be seen in the west at one clear point. The trail leads downhill on St. Anton Way to Archibald Way and then onto Lakeside Road. It is well signed at each turn. (New additions to the Whistler parks system are being built by the developer of Blueberry Hill. Both a trail past the golf course and a small beach park at the foot of the hill on Alta Lake will be open in 1992.)

There is a small point of public access to Alta Lake (once called Summit Lake) at the foot of Carleton Way off Lakeside Road where it winds south towards Lakeside Park. This is a good location for boats or windsurfers to launch. There is no parking at this launch, but there's plenty of room for vehicles at Lakeside Park, one block past here.

LAKESIDE PARK   Lakeside Park is an open area on the southeast side of Alta Lake. A lawn runs down to the beach with its two L-shaped docks. There are six well-spaced picnic tables, most with their own barbecues. There is no lifeguard, and dogs are not allowed on the beach. The Whistler Outdoor Experience Co. (phone 932-3589) operates a boat and windsurfer rental here and offers guided tours of the lake and the River of Golden Dreams.

WAYSIDE PARK   The Valley trail climbs the hill behind Lakeside Park and rounds the corner past Alta Vista Point, reaching Wayside Park after a short descent through the trees. This is a smaller park than Lakeside. Four picnic tables, each with its own barbecue, sit on a sloped hillside overlooking the south end of Alta Lake. There is a modest beach with an open lawn above for sunbathing. A dock is moored just far enough offshore to make swimmers appreciate reaching it after a plunge in the cold waters of Alta Lake. Canoe and Laser sailboat rentals are handled from a small boathouse. (They are slightly less expensive here than at Lakeside Park.) On Sunday afternoons during the spring and summer months, sailing races are held at Wayside, following a slalom course to the north end of the lake and back. You can either rent a Laser or take your own if you wish to enter. You can see a dozen or so Lasers chasing each other during the races, sometimes led by a windsurfer.

As the Valley trail heads south of Wayside Park, across from the Nordic Estates and Whistler Highlands neighbourhoods, it passes the south end of Alta Lake. A handful of old cabins nestle beside the railway tracks. They are reminiscent of a time before 1965 when the only access to Whistler was on the Pacific Great Eastern (now B.C. Rail).

NITA LAKE   The Valley trail rounds the rocky corners of Nita Lake, crossing Whistler Creek on its east side. There are two picnic tables here and a small gravel beach built up by the annual freshet in the creek when the snow melts on the mountainside above.

At the south end of Nita Lake, next to the Whistler Tennis Club courts, are two of the oldest cabins in the valley. One of them, built in 1933 by pioneers Russ Jordan and Bill Bailiff on land purchased from Harry Horstman, hosted visitors until 1967. Today's owners, John and Kay Taylor, maintain Jordan's Hunting Lodge in its original condition.

Next to Jordan's is the Whistler train station, hidden behind a small evergreen ridge. The enclosed station and platform are located on a curve; the train makes its appearance at the very last moment before coming to a stop. The passenger train arrives from Vancouver shortly after 10 AM each morning on its way north; return service is scheduled for 6:15 PM, with a later departure in summer. Check the schedule with B.C. Rail (phone 631-3500). Black cottonwoods beside Jordan Creek, which drains south from Nita Lake, offer shelter if you are waiting for the train on warm summer afternoons. The view from here is of the

Alta Lake Park's fanciful playhouse and swing set were created with small children in mind.

famous downhill course on Whistler Mountain's west face. A small trail runs behind the train station over to Alpha Lake Park.

It's a 5-minute walk from the train station to the Silver Bullet ski lift at the foot of Whistler Mountain. Taxi and bus service are also available from here; both meet the train. There is a pay phone by the train station.

ALPHA LAKE   Alpha Lake Park is beside one of the oldest neighbourhoods in the valley, Whistler Creek. Squaw Valley Crescent and Lake Placid Road are two of the original streets in modern Whistler. A great deal of new construction around the east shore of Alpha Lake attests to the revitalization of this side of Whistler Mountain, which was eclipsed for a time in the 1980s by the development of the village.

The park features some whimsical architecture, including a hobbit-sized playhouse and swing for young children, and the bridge of yellow cedar over Jordan Creek. (These creations, and other art nouveau-style woodwork around Whistler, were crafted by Eric Scragg.) A tennis court, canoe and dinghy rentals, and the Taylor Nature Walk augment the beach, picnic tables and barbecues. Alpha Lake is very irregularly shaped, making it enjoyable to explore by boat. Circle around the island on which a family has built one of the most admired cottages in all of Whistler, linked to the mainland by a private bridge.

At publication the Valley trail ends at Alpha Lake. If you wish to go farther, follow the rough trail and the train tracks around the west side of Alpha Lake until they link with Alta Lake Road, or ride out through the Baseline neighbourhood to Highway 99 and around onto Alta Lake Road. The road into Whistler originally came from Function Junction at the town's south end and divided at the south end of Alpha Lake. The old road to Function Junction now serves as a bicycle path. It crosses Millar Creek, which drains out of Alpha Lake's south end.

ALTA LAKE ROAD   While not a part of the Valley trail, Alta Lake Road links Alpha Park with Rainbow Park and the Valley trail at the northwest end of Alta Lake, 3 mi. (5 km) apart. The road runs along the west side of the valley, giving limited access to Alpha Lake before climbing the ridge above it and Nita Lake. North of Rainbow the road runs 3 mi. (5 km) to the neighbourhood of Alpine Meadows, changes its name to Rainbow Drive for a short distance, then rejoins Highway 99.

If you'd just like to go boating, head for Pine Point Park, a little dock for fishing at the south end of Alpha Lake. It's the best place to launch a boat directly from your vehicle onto the lake. To reach it, drive around from Highway 99 on Alta Lake Road until you reach the railway crossing. The turnoff to the park is just to the right of the tracks before you cross them.

If you're not stopping at the park, continue across the tracks. The road begins to climb steeply up Cardiac Hill. Running off to the left of the pavement is a rough gravel road leading up to a popular climbing location called Cardiac Bluff. It continues north above the hydro lines, rejoining Alta Lake Road opposite the entrance to Rainbow Park.

Where Alta Lake Road reaches the ridge above Nita Lake there is a fine viewpoint with a pull-off beside the road. You can park your car here. An interpretive sign, beautifully painted by local artist Isobel MacLaurin, details some of the highlights of the view across the valley. Whistler Mountain is the centrepiece here. Similar interpretive signs are posted at many other scenic locations in the valley, including one farther along Alta Lake Road.

A short way south of Rainbow Park on Alta Lake Road is the Whistler Hostel. Years ago it operated as Harrop's Lodge; in the late 1960s it housed the first ski instructors employed by the Whistler Mountain Ski School. It was purchased by the Canadian Youth Hostel Association in 1972. The turnoff to the hostel is well marked from the highway. Drive down and park in front of a large shed. The hostel itself is on a point of land on the lakeshore. To reach it you must descend a staircase and cross the railway tracks. This is one of the best views on the lake, because the hostel is one of the few properties on the west side of the lake located on the water; the rest of the cabins and homes are on the hillside above the railway tracks.

If you wish to make a round-trip of the Valley trail and Alta Lake Road by bicycle, I recommend this approach: take the Valley trail out to Rainbow Park, follow Alta Lake Road south to Highway 99, swing around north on the highway for a short distance. and then hook up with the Valley trail at Alpha Lake. The reasoning is simple: near the south end of Alta Lake Road there is a great downhill run that will be more enjoyable than climbing uphill in the opposite direction.

North of Rainbow Park, Alta Lake Road follows the ridge above the wildlife refuge (there is no public access to the refuge, which is a large wetland for nesting birds) towards 21-Mile Creek. Along the way there is another pull-off and an interpretive sign. A short distance uphill on the opposite side of the road is the Whistler Cemetery. This quiet spot is the resting place of several Whistler pioneers, including Myrtle Philip and her sister Jean Tapley. Dave Murray, who achieved so much on behalf of amateur skiers after a successful career representing Canada on the World Cup circuit, is also buried here.

The well-marked trail to Rainbow Falls begins just up the road from the cemetery. There is a parking lot for visitors. You can make a quick circuit by taking the trail up to the falls, then descending the gravel road that comes out onto Alta Lake Road next to the cemetery. Just before Alta Lake Road enters the Alpine Meadows neighbourhood, there is a well-marked entrance to the Valley trail on the east side of the road. Meadow Park is a short distance north of here.

No matter in which direction you follow the Valley trail, you will find a place in which to relax while enjoying the outdoor scenery. Part of the fun is watching families at play—a rare sight in the city, but one that defines Whistler's appeal.

13 | RIVER OF GOLDEN DREAMS (ALTA CREEK)

BIRD-WATCHING ◄
CYCLING ◄
PADDLING ◄
PICNICKING ◄
VIEWPOINTS ◄

Alex Philip not only ran Rainbow Lodge on Alta Lake with his wife, Myrtle, he also found time to write two novels with western settings (one, *The Crimson West*, was turned into a screenplay for a romantic Hollywood production). He also used his literary skills to add a poetic touch to the small stream that flows between Alta and Green lakes, dubbing it the River of Golden Dreams in honour of the honeymooning couples who would paddle it while staying at Rainbow or one of the other lodges on the lake. The stream is officially named Alta Creek, but as a tribute to Alex the municipality of Whistler refers to it as the River of Golden Dreams on signs and maps.

Rainbow Lodge was destroyed by fire in 1977, but a park has taken its place. Couples still launch small boats from here or from several other locations on Alta Lake, paddling down the creek with pleasure in mind. This is a leisurely way to spend several hours, drifting with the current, hardly having to put your paddle in the water in order to glide along.

To find the entrance to the River of Golden Dreams, head for the small bay at Alta Lake's north end. There is no sign of a channel flowing out of the lake until you have almost reached the shore. Tall reeds form the perimeter of the bay. Just when you think you should have taken another approach, perhaps closer to the lake's northeastern side, a narrow opening leads you into a winding channel. (See Valley Trail chapter for map of this area.)

This is the beginning of the River of Golden Dreams. From here there is a great view to the west of the peak of Rainbow Mountain. You can hear many birds call while paddling along in the springtime; some of these are nesting in the reeds beside the channel. As you pass by you may startle them into performing their distress routine, hoping to distract your attention from their young.

Near the outset of the narrow, winding channel, you pass a pleasant little dock with racks of canoes next to a private condominium. Paddle under the wooden bridge nearby. (The path crossing the bridge is part of the Valley trail to Rainbow Park.) Just beyond this point you must portage over a small concrete weir, built to compensate for a sudden drop in the river. This is easily negotiated, as the builders kept river travel in mind when they designed it.

From here the river parallels the B.C. Rail tracks for a straight shallow stretch before merging with the outflow of water from 21-Mile Creek. Water levels in the channel are high enough in spring to allow passage. Later in the year you may have to get out of your canoe for part of the distance if it bottoms out. With this in mind, wear an old pair of runners in which you can hop out into the water when needed. The river bottom is mostly sand.

The river becomes much wider and better defined from here north. Be prepared to negotiate several tricky turns for a short distance as the increased volume of water moves along more quickly. There are no rocky rapids, but an occasional floating snag or submerged branch might catch you momentarily.

Almost as soon as the two waterways merge, you pass under a large pedestrian bridge next to where the Valley trail crosses the B.C. Rail tracks adjacent to a large gravel pit. The river bends around several corners beside the tracks, as the roofs of nearby homes in the Whistler Cay neighbourhood appear above the tall growth on the riverbank. North of here the railway and river diverge, with the tracks running off on the east side of the valley while the river cuts over to the west. The river widens even more as it passes beneath a series of hydro towers. Blackcomb Peak is prominent to the east as the houses drop from sight and the vista becomes more open. Pairs of yellow warblers flit from branch to branch on the red willow overhanging the banks. In summer you may have to portage over several sturdy beaver dams; high water covers them until late spring when levels begin to drop.

The river flows beside the Valley trail in several places as it moves away from the hydro lines. Thus begins the most pleasant stretch of river. One of the best views appears as you round one of its bends: the high vegetation suddenly thins out to reveal a panorama of peaks stretching from Blackcomb and Wedge mountains all the way north to Mount Currie. For the next half-hour the current carries you gently onward with this mountainscape rising before you.

Meadow Park appears on the west bank of the river with its picnic tables and fireplaces at riverside. Just past here the remains of an old wooden bridge stand as a reminder of a time when it was the principal means of crossing. You are close to Green Lake now. If the water levels in the river are high, prepare to take your boat out at either Meadow Park or the boat launch beside the log footbridge after you pass under the

Highway 99 bridge. The current picks up as the river approaches Green Lake. It's a challenge to work your way back upstream early in the summer; by August water levels have usually dropped to the point where you can paddle to Green Lake and back upstream without fighting the current.

The river snakes back and forth through several final turns before it reaches the lake. Tall Sitka spruce line the banks. This last section is special; don't pass it up unless you are really pressed for time. Reaching Green Lake triggers a great feeling of release. As the river enters the lake its colour deepens from clear gold to green. Much of this change occurs as you paddle over the gravel bar.

Green Lake lies open before you, inviting exploration. It takes an hour to reach the north end, depending in which direction the wind is blowing. If you visit the lake in early spring or late fall, watch for the white swans that spend several days here while on migration. You can count on them being here on their way north when the ice goes out in April; they return on October 30, almost always to the day.

If you took your boat out back at the bridge, you can still explore along the banks of the river to see where it enters Green Lake. Members of the Whistler Off-Road Cycling Association have cleared parts of this trail for riders, put down gravel, and marked the way in places with orange tapes. The rough river trail leads off to the left of the Valley trail beside the bridge. Right beside it is a large parking area in front of the Whistler Heli-ski cabin. (Out of deference to trail users the municipality permits flights only during winter months.) If you are not planning to paddle back to Alta Lake, this is a good place to arrange to be picked up. Another plan is to leave a bicycle here before you start; drive your vehicle and boat over to Rainbow Park, paddle downstream to Green Lake, then ride back along the Valley trail to reclaim your vehicle, returning to retrieve your boat by driving west on Alta Lake Road to Highway 99, a short distance north of the River of Golden Dreams.

14 | ALPINE MEADOWS AND EMERALD ESTATES

BIRD-WATCHING ◄
CYCLING ◄
HIKING ◄
SWIMMING ◄
VIEWPOINTS ◄
WALKING ◄

When you begin to adventure around Whistler after the snow melts, on foot or by bicycle, there are always more trails to explore than you originally bargained for. Many are old roads left from the days when logging was going strong on the valley slopes. A number of Whistler neighbourhoods have intentionally created watershed zones in clear-cut areas above the highest streets. Second-growth is beginning to noticeably re-cover the scarred landscape in these watersheds.

Alpine Meadows and Emerald Estates are the two most northerly neighbourhoods in Whistler. With a little effort you can reach panoramic viewpoints from the old roads above them. Looking out over the valley is as good a geography lesson as you can experience, next to paragliding or flying. A camera can capture much of the expanse; at certain spots your eyes will hardly be big enough to take it all in. What you see is Whistler evolving before you. (See Valley Trail chapter for map of this area.)

Everywhere leading off the dirt roads around the watersheds are bike trails. Mountain bikers are in the vanguard when it comes to creating new trails around Whistler. Off-road riders confront the physical challenge of the sport while pumping their new-age mules to places of great beauty. You don't have to be on wheels to enjoy these trails, though some are steeper than you would want to attempt, even on foot. Others follow gentle old logging roads. In Whistler, mountain bike riders keep these roads open as trails; those on foot help them too. We all have the same objective: those quiet, enchanting places just above the neighbourhoods of Whistler.

ALPINE MEADOWS Reaching the top of Alpine Meadows is quite straightforward. The turnoff from Highway 99 puts you on Alpine Way. Drive along this paved street to the very top and park. Follow a dirt road uphill on foot or by bicycle from here; within minutes you will reach

"Rick's Roost," a viewpoint named for local photographer Rick Flebbe. You'll know the spot when a view of the valley stretching from Green to Alta lakes opens up suddenly on your right. Measuring your position at the Roost against the slopes of Blackcomb and Whistler mountains across the way helps you gauge your altitude above the valley. Whether you are a first-time visitor or a Whistler pioneer, the view never loses its freshness. It seems that you can see everything that's happening in the valley at once.

Now that you've reached the Roost, you can treat yourself to a leisurely walk back down through Alpine Meadows admiring the variety of abodes, from large gasthaus lodgings to the little caboose tucked away at the corner of Alpine and Drifter Way. Or continue adventuring on the upper slopes, where you can spend an hour or an entire day exploring old and new trails.

Above the Roost the road climbs steadily into the watershed. The first two side roads on the left lead over to a small creek feeding down the south side of Alpine Meadows and into the River of Golden Dreams. Several concrete dams regulate the flow of the creek, channelling some of it into water towers for the neighbourhood's use. There is also a satellite-dish communication centre nearby. The roads are kept in good shape so service vehicles can drive in.

Not far above the Roost, the dirt road deteriorates quickly to an alder-lined path. It heads uphill on a moderate incline, with level spots in places, curving one way and then the other. Stick with this; you will soon reach a clearing where Lost Lake comes into view on the opposite side of the valley. From below, this lake is hidden in the forest; you have to reach a higher elevation than the Roost to see it.

Concealed in the trees nearby to the north of the trail is 19-Mile Creek. You can see the outline of its path by the old-growth on each side of the canyon as it drops down through the heart of Alpine Meadows. After the creek passes under the Highway 99 bridge it runs downstream past a stand of tall black cottonwood, then fans out into a small delta. It's almost impossible to tell where it makes its entrance into Green Lake. On the cleared hillside are signs of a fire that raced through after it was logged.

Watch for the trail to divide. One branch continues north towards 19-Mile Creek while the other makes a sharp left turn. A small rock cairn stands in the middle of the path, barely noticeable at first. This is your cue to take the trail to the left. (If you miss the cairn and keep on going straight ahead in an attempt to reach 19-Mile Creek you may find that the path soon becomes so overgrown with alder that you must stoop down to get through it. The alder are bowed over by the weight of snow in winter, and gradually rise during summer, clearing the path for easier exploration. The path itself takes on the appearance of an old creekbed.

The trail around Lost Lake is a good place to stretch your legs in any season.

It does eventually lead to the banks of 19- Mile Creek, but you may need a machete to clear the way. It isn't all bad, as there are some clearings with good views along the way, especially from the hillside above the path. Blue tapes mark the way, showing that someone has been here before you. Large piles of bear feces indicate that humans aren't the only ones to use this path—sing as you walk along so you don't take anyone by surprise.)

The trail that goes to the left at the cairn leads upwards onto a level ridge. The farther along this ridge you travel, the better the views become. A moderate climb through open brush leads to the old-growth forest above; along the way you pass more fully developed second-growth than previously encountered. This trail often shows signs of bike treads.

After you have been on the trail above Alpine Meadows for about 1 hour, you'll reach a double cairn, one on each side of the path as if this were a gateway. The trail divides here. You may be satisfied to have found the views from this ridge and be ready to retrace your steps. Or you can carry on, making a loop over to 21-Mile Creek (several hours away from Alpine Meadows) and back along Alta Lake Road. The branch leading uphill has been intentionally blocked by several old branches. These signs speak volumes: if you wish to continue farther, take the open trail to the left.

Blue tapes help guide your course when the trail gets overgrown. Also watch for signs that bikes have been through here. Where a mountain bike crosses a blow-down the chain often cuts into the wood, leaving an open red mark that is very helpful in identifying the pathway. These slashes are as evident as the more traditional orange metal markers nailed to tree trunks. With time, many more tires and boot soles will establish a better path.

The open trail passes through old-growth forest for 10 to 15 minutes. The soft ground bounces under your feet. After the logged area you climbed through on your way up here, you'll find this a pleasant place to be, sharing the silence of the forest with the occasional chickadee. You can easily strike up a conversation with these chatty little birds, who will respond to a repetition of their call, *chick-a-dee-dee-dee*.

From the old-growth forest you now emerge into the open once again. A small stream descends through the clearing, coming down from the side of Rainbow Mountain. Cross this stream on a series of logs. As you move south along a ridge, you overlook the last section of 21-Mile Creek as it flows down towards Alta Lake. Your only clue to 21-Mile Creek's course higher up the mountain is the line of old-growth flanking its banks.

A second small stream appears on the open slope, and beside it some very large stumps, more than 6 ft. (2 m) in diameter. With all the low-lying huckleberry bushes around there will be good fall colour here after the first frost. The ground in late spring and early summer is quite mucky around the stream for a short distance, then the trail rises to another small clearing. Looking across the valley you can see that you are at approximately the same elevation as mid-station on Blackcomb and Whistler mountains. Enjoy the view, then watch your footing; it gets muddy again for the next 5 to 10 minutes. The trail doubles as a creekbed as it descends, meeting up with an old road. Waterproof footwear will make this section of the trail much more enjoyable. Thick alder brush borders the trail. Its growth seems to be regulated by an invisible elevation line above which it doesn't thrive.

Another small cairn appears, along with a series of white tapes. From here you can see a low concrete watershed building on the south side of 21-Mile Creek, with Mount Sproatt rising above. The closer the trail gets to the creek, the narrower it becomes. Rather than continue up the valley on the open trail, bear left at each junction. Tape markers help lead you on. (There is no place to cross 21- Mile Creek at any point above here.) Descend over some fallen logs and you'il find another cairn waiting for you. Again, chain marks exposing red wood on otherwise blackened logs will help you decide where to proceed.

The trail descends steadily from here to Alta Lake Road. It reaches a clearing where there are a dozen tall snags still standing among the living old-growth forest. Moss covers much of the rock face. 21-Mile Creek is quite close at hand now; there are exhilarating views of Rainbow Mountain above to the west. Enjoy this; the views begin to disappear below this clearing as you descend towards the valley floor. You may spot hikers on the opposite side of 21-Mile Creek on the first stages of the trail leading up to Rainbow Mountain.

As you cross the ridge watch for pink tapes leading down towards the creek. Finding your way is somewhat tricky, and the going is steep. A triangular cairn appears at one of the best viewpoints on the entire journey. Green Lake is visible in the distance, and in the foreground is a stand of tall old-growth forest. From the cairn there is only one choice of descent, off to your right as you face east; all other directions lead to impassable cliff faces. The next 165 ft. (50 m) is the steepest section. The ground underneath your feet is soft and loamy. Sturdy old-growth will help break your slide should you get going too fast. You may wonder as you descend how anyone could do it carrying a bike.

The forest is draped in long wisps of moss. You are quite close to the creek now, and the sound of its rushing water rises above the canyon walls. Unfortunately there is no view of Rainbow Falls from this side.

The trail improves from here down to the road. Tape in a variety of colours leads down to a very innocent-looking, barely noticeable entrance to Alta Lake Road. This is directly across the road from the large parking lot built in 1991 to hold the cars of hikers using the Rainbow trail. (An old road leads through the forest beside 21-Mile Creek below Alta Lake Road. It begins where a wooden gate bars vehicle access from the Rainbow parking lot.)

As you head north towards Alpine Meadows along Alta Lake Road, watch for a small creek that passes under the highway through a culvert; this is the same stream that made parts of the trail mucky high above on the ridge. A trail heads uphill beside the stream to a small salmon enhancement project. On the other side of the road numerous bike paths descend to meet the Valley trail. The forest below the road is a warren of old logging roads and newer bike trails. Watch for the well-marked paved entrance to the Valley trail. Directly across the road from this entrance, leading uphill, is a rough bike trail. Follow it north for 10 minutes as it heads over to the small creek descending from the Alpine Meadows watershed. There is a crossing that will bring you out onto Forest Ridge Drive. Turn left onto Fissile Lane. This leads back onto Alpine Way; you are now within minutes of the trailhead at Rick's Roost, having come full circle. On foot this will have taken you 4 to 5 hours to complete.

19-MILE CREEK   The trail between 21-Mile and 19-Mile creeks was developed by the Whistler Off-Road Cycling Association. With time it will link with other such trails, eventually forming a subalpine route around the whole Whistler Valley. The trails on both sides of 19-Mile Creek will eventually be cleared and linked up. As it stands, the old road up the north side of the creek is overgrown but passable.

To find it, take Alpine Way from Highway 99 to Valley Drive. Turn right, cross a bridge over 19-Mile Creek, and follow it to its end. You'll see a gate barring vehicle access into the watershed. Follow the road beyond two green water towers. (Joining the old road here is a path that leads to nearby Mountainview Drive.) The road into the watershed begins to deteriorate above the towers while climbing steadily uphill. You will soon reach the open slopes above Alpine where logging has cleared wide areas. You won't be able to get close to 19-Mile Creek until much higher up the mountainside; take a machete to clear the way. The views from this side of the creek are much less stimulating than those from Rick's Roost.

EMERALD ESTATES   The watershed above Whistler's most northern neighbourhood holds something unique: a small, unnamed lake. In summer, as water levels drop, it appears that there are two lakes side by side. You can walk or ride to the lake along a rough road and trail; alder will be in your face for the last part of the trail. It's an easy 30-minute walk from either of two entrances to the watershed off Emerald Drive, the highest paved street in the neighbourhood. It's not really worth driving to Emerald to find, but if you've biked over from other parts of Whistler, or paddled up Green Lake to land at Emerald Estates, this is an idyllic picnic location, especially if you have the lake to yourself. In summer a raft is anchored in the middle of the larger part of the lake. The residents of Emerald have a love affair with this little lake and like to keep it clean. You'll find the trail litter-free—do help it stay that way.

On the way to one of the watershed entrances, make sure you see the famous Mushroom House of Whistler at the corner of Pinecone and Emerald Drive. For owner Zube Aylward, building the house has been a labour of love since 1980. Flashed in copper, with a cedar-shake roof, this art nouveau-influenced home was severely damaged by a fire in late

August 1991. While the top of the house was almost completely destroyed, much of the remainder is intact. Assisted by donations from local admirers, Aylward hopes to restore the house to its former glory, at which time public tours will resume.

To the right of Pinecone, Emerald Drive climbs a short distance towards Deerhorn. Some of the steepest staircases in Whistler rise to homes perched above this road. Watch for a short, rough, steep ascent to a reservoir in the Emerald watershed on your left. Climb to the left of it to find the trail to the lake. Stay right at all turns and you'll soon be there.

An easier approach is to go left on Emerald Drive at Pinecone. The paved road winds its way past more interesting homes. Next to 9515 Emerald is a watershed marker. From here a rough road rises through young second-growth to a ridge, where it meets the trail to the lake on its left. At several places on this road you get good views of the mountains on the east side of the valley. Here at the top of Green Lake there are better views of Mount Weart and the Owls, a volcanic ridge fanned out between two rocky horns. Despite the low elevation, from here you get some of the best views in the valley of Blackcomb.

Each of these routes feeds into the lake trail after 15 minutes. Near the lake the trail divides. Take the right fork, the more open of the two choices. (The trail to the left circles the lake on a very old road that ends below a ridge at the lake's south end. Although the lake is close at hand, it's never in view.) In a couple of minutes you will reach the lake. Several paths lead up through the open forest to reach the smaller section of the lake. The main path leads down to the large section.

Sounds rising from the valley, like the trucks shifting gears on Highway 99, disappear at the lake. It's tucked in behind a ridge of old-growth that acts as a shield. A steep slope of volcanic scree covers the western shoreline. When peace and quiet permeate the scene you'll get a show of birdlife: kingfishers work the lake, hovering and diving two or three times on one pass before settling onto a branch, calling out triumphantly. A family of mergansers glide around the perimeter, dabbling for tasty vegetation. Even though the chicks look fluffy, they can dive and paddle adeptly, especially at the call of their mother. If you sit still, a ground feeder such as a tiny black-headed junco or a much larger woodpecker will hop through the underbrush past you. The play of wind and sunlight on the blue water is hypnotic. The surface shimmers, a sparkling patina shifting like accordion bellows squeezed one way and then the other. On days like this, you become one with the outdoor magic of Whistler.

15 | BLACKCOMB

Blackcomb opened for skiing in 1980. From its inception in 1975 the ski facility has been closely identified with Nancy Greene Raine, Canada's world champion ski racer who won one gold medal and one silver at the 1968 Winter Olympics in Grenoble, France. She's easy to spot on Blackcomb and still the one to beat when it comes to non-stop peak-to-valley descents.

The president of Blackcomb, Hugh Smythe, was one of Whistler Mountain's original employees when it opened in 1966. Smythe has supervised a very aggressive expansion plan that has seen Blackcomb evolve from junior status to Whistler Mountain's formidable chief competitor. Longtime visitors have reaped the benefits of this decade-old rivalry. In the minds of many, Blackcomb is the best thing that happened to Whistler—both the mountain and village.

As well as offering a wide expanse of varied terrain, Blackcomb has an attitude towards public relations that makes visiting the mountain a pleasure. Mountain Hosts is a 20-member team of volunteers who accompany skiers wishing an introduction to Blackcomb. Simply request assistance at the guest services desk in the Merlin Lodge at the base of the mountain. There is no charge for this tour.

Now, it may not be apparent at first why you would want to be chaperoned around the trails, especially if you have skied Blackcomb in previous years. But with the operational expansion the mountain undergoes year after year, I find that I need a crash course at the start of each season on the new runs woven into the network of existing trails. With Mountain Hosts as guides you quickly learn how you can make your way around the mountain, moving from lift to lift, making the most economical use of your time. Rather than spend time waiting in line, wondering where to head next, let them help you sort out your options.

There are many possibilities for skiers at any ability level to enjoy Blackcomb from top to bottom. The best views, of course, exist on top. But no skier needs to feel deprived of the panorama of the Coast Mountains. While more advanced skiers may choose to make their way down via a variety of intermediate and black diamond routes from the summit of 7th Heaven, there are also two easy ski-outs. One is called simply "Easiest Route." The other is the gentle "Hot Rocks Traverse" linking the Horstman Hut at the top of 7th Heaven to the Crystal Hut on the ridge above the Blackcomb Glacier. Along the way you take in some truly expansive scenery. The view is spectacular, but even more important is the chance to check beforehand which trails are most congested. On the slopes between the Crystal Hut and Rendezvous Lodge, clusters of skiers stand out in miniature, populating the mountain like figures in a Grandma Moses painting.

From the top of the Crystal Ridge a gentle trail called Ridge Runner connects with the Blackcomb Glacier ski-out, eventually leading to mid-station. For part of the way you can sit back on your skis, admiring the girth of the old-growth Douglas fir beside the trail. If you want more of a challenge, the broad top of Ridge Runner holds plenty of powder and you can ski it for all it's worth. Snowboarders will find plenty of excitement on the escarpments of the ridge. Blackcomb has trail markers for snowboarders, directing them to a half-pipe just below the junction of the Jersey Cream quad-chair and the Crystal Ridge lift. Sound complex? It's actually a breeze to fit the puzzle together once you've been led through the maze by a Mountain Host.

Blackcomb Mountain offers the only summer glacier skiing of any mountain in North America. At present the summer ski and snowboard camps vie with recreational skiers for space on the Horstman Glacier.

CYCLING ON BLACKCOMB   Skiing is only one part of the year-round recreational picture in the Whistler Valley. Mountain biking has arrived in a big way on both Whistler and Blackcomb mountains. Although you may have huffed and puffed along some of the valley trails as a warm-up, nothing can quite prepare you for a downhill run on these rough mountain roads.

Mountain biking requires special skills that many riders have not acquired even after years on city and country roads. The roads down Blackcomb and Whistler Mountain are unrivalled for challenge and variety. Be sure to read carefully the instructions for bike riders posted next to the lifts. They include pointers such as staying to the inside corner on turns to reduce the risk of a spill. Wear protective clothing even if the warm summer sun encourages you to remove a layer or two. If you do have a spill, long sleeves and pant legs will lessen the chance of your taking some of the mountain home under your skin.

Any skier will agree that Blackcomb's 7th Heaven is well named.

Check with the mountains ahead of time to compare temperatures in the valley with those on top. For weather reports on Blackcomb, call 932-4211 (from Vancouver, 687-7507). You'll be surprised how the air changes from comfortable to cool on your way up the lift. You won't get warm coming downhill, either, as much of your time will be spent braking and steering without much need for pumping.

If you want to test your ability to handle the roads on Blackcomb or Whistler, try some of the gravel roads around Lost Lake first. Once you're confident enough to tackle the mountain, take time to get to know the runs before going all out.

Cyclists first had the thrill of wheeling down Blackcomb's twisting service roads in 1988. That first year only groups escorted by a Blackcomb guide were allowed access. (Whistler Mountain still maintains a similar policy.) After seeing the demand, Blackcomb changed its approach: for the price of a lift ticket plus a bike charge, riders can enjoy unlimited use of seven designated trails. There's a *Hiker/Biker Trail Guide* published to help visitors find their way around the mountain. Helmets are mandatory, for very good reasons, and can be rented at the Blackcomb Ski & Sport shop next to the lift. Bikes are also available by the hour or day.

The lifts start running at 7:30 AM, catering for the most part to the summer skiers who line up in the warm sun in full winter attire. It can be cool on the Horstman Glacier where they are headed. Snow from late spring storms may still be packed down at elevations just above the Solar

Coaster chairlift. It will often be late July before all the trails in the higher alpine area are snow-free. You can choose to get off midway up Blackcomb at the top of the Wizard Express or continue on to the top on the Solar Coaster. You may find that the runs from the top to mid-station are more enjoyable and slightly less demanding. In that case, stay on the top half rather than making a complete descent of the mountain each time.

Chubby marmots sunbathe on the hot rocks beside the road in front of the Rendezvous Lodge. The road begins from the top of the Solar Coaster chairlift. Almost immediately you begin using your brakes as the bike picks up speed more quickly than you may have bargained for. There's not much time to get used to being in the saddle before you have to be alert and sitting as far back on your seat as you can. The designated routes are well marked, with caution signs where the going gets tough. Take along a pair of gloves, as your hands will be absorbing a tremendous impact from the rough road. In some places the surface is gravelled, requiring a constant application of the brakes, whereas in other sections it's hard-packed dirt. Dirt is easier to manoeuvre on, and it also allows you to let the bike run free with less emphasis on braking. You'll need to pull over after a while just to allow your hands to relax for a few minutes. It's refreshing to let your eyes drink in a view of the surrounding mountains instead of concentrating on the road falling away in front of you.

If you're wondering what to do if you have equipment trouble way up there, note that regular bike patrols give you the same reassurance that an automobile club membership provides. Fully equipped with tools and first-aid supplies, the bike patrol will be most appreciated by those who rent or ride borrowed bikes and are perhaps less acquainted with simple repair techniques.

There are two halves to the descent down Blackcomb. From the top of the Solar Coaster to mid-station, the road drops sharply through a series of switchbacks after an initial glide down towards the 7th Heaven chairlift. Views of the Singing Pass trail, far below in the Fitzsimmons Valley, predominate for the first while.

From mid-station to the valley, the road widens with longer straightaways. Surprisingly, some of the steepest sections of the entire trail occur just before the maintenance yards. The pavement begins below the yards; from here on down, the ride is a breeze. The corners are banked, and your bike seems to know its own way back to the bottom of the Wizard Express, where you began an hour earlier. Your ticket allows you as many runs as you can fit into a day (it's possible to make five or six full-length runs). The lifts close to riders at 4 PM, allowing the bike patrol to make a last sweep of the trails. They don't want to leave anyone stranded on the mountain overnight.

There are some riders who disdain the lifts and pump up the road under their own steam. There ought to be free burgers on top for those who make it all the way. The road up Blackcomb begins at the bottom of the Wizard Express lift; you can also bike up the paved road to the maintenance yards above Blackcomb Way and join the trail there.

You don't need a bike in order to explore Blackcomb Mountain in the summer. There are a variety of walking trails in the alpine region of 7th Heaven where you can only go on foot. You can choose to explore on your own, following the trail guide, or take one of the free tours of the mountain, guided by naturalists, that are offered several times daily.

Your visit doesn't have to end at sunset. A local astronomer leads stargazing sessions on Saturday evenings in summer on the deck of the Rendezvous Lodge. Check with Blackcomb for exact times.

16 | RAINBOW MOUNTAIN

CAMPING ◄
FISHING ◄
HIKING ◄
SWIMMING ◄
VIEWPOINTS ◄
WALKING ◄

In many ways the hike into Rainbow Mountain is the perfect counter-part to the Singing Pass trail. They begin on opposite sides of Whistler Valley, Singing Pass in the east and Rainbow in the west. By the time you reach the top of Singing Pass you see Rainbow Mountain in all its glory, and vice versa.

The Rainbow Lake trail begins from Alta Lake Road and is well marked. (See Valley Trail chapter for map of this area.) There is parking on both sides of the road next to 21-Mile Creek. At this point the creek is close to the end of its run down the mountain. Before it was diverted by construction of the railway, it emptied into Alta Lake; now it flows into the River of Golden Dreams (Alta Creek) and from there into Green Lake.

RAINBOW FALLS   You can make a little or a lot out of this 10-mi. (16-km) round-trip trail. If you don't have a day to spend doing the round-trip in summer, or if snow conditions make it impossible to reach higher elevations at other times of the year, you can still enjoy a visit to the waterfall close to the trailhead. It's only a 15-minute climb to see it. Two trails, one old and one new, parallel each other as they climb to the falls. The old one runs beside the creek, then climbs through a series of switchbacks in the original-growth forest. It's fun to take a bicycle up this trail. The new one is more of a scramble, up the bank beside the trailhead marker and across a watershed road. (Gated at the bottom, this road leads up from the nearby Whistler Cemetery to a concrete pump-house just above the falls.) No matter which of the two you decide to take, you will have to descend a moderately steep slope to get a good view of the falls just below the crest of the watershed road. Water levels are highest in late May, making this one of the best times to see the frothing creek in action. The canyon through which it flows is full of smooth boulders and thick moss. A relentless hypnotic liquid sound shuts out all

After a long uphill hike, the view of Mount Wedge from Rainbow Lake is your reward.

else; you'll come away refreshed from this meditative experience.

Take another few steps to the road above the falls to enjoy a good view east up the Fitzsimmons Valley separating Blackcomb and Whistler mountains. If you climb just a little bit higher above the pumphouse, you can see Green Lake to the north. Just beside the pumphouse a 1.2-mi. (2-km) trail runs downhill to Rainbow Park on nearby Alta Lake.

RAINBOW LAKE The trail above the pumphouse is in rough shape for a short distance as it crosses a badly eroded section of the hillside. It then begins to climb along an old logging road overgrown with alder on each side. The branches gradually straighten up during summer months after being bowed down by the weight of snow in winter. Wear some eye protection in spring months.

You're in for a laugh after 30 minutes of this. Standing there in a clearing is a bright blue bike rack. It seems an odd item to encounter in the wilderness. A sign posted beside it reminds those who have punished themselves by cycling to this point that they should ride no farther. Spare the fragile alpine and lock up here. You can take your dog, though, because this isn't part of Garibaldi Provincial Park.

Take a look around here. There haven't been many views until this point, and there won't be many more for another bit. Put up with it; you will be more than justly rewarded in another hour. Across the valley on Blackcomb's west face you can see the Showcase T-Bar on the Horstman Glacier. Below it are the distinctive features of the famous Saudan Couloir extreme-ski chute, framed by the shoulders of the canyon above 21-Mile Creek. This is a pretty place to be.

The trail beyond the bike rack gets rough. It's really nothing more than a narrow trench that has been notched in the earth by an active spring creek. Put your head down and do it. In 15 minutes you'll have put the climb through the lower slopes behind you. You now enter the graceful old-growth forest. The trail consists of well-tracked forest floor supplemented by boardwalks, small bridges, and fallen logs notched into steps and staircases. Primarily Douglas fir and western hemlock, this forest also has occasional stands of red cedar.

One particularly pleasant spot occurs just past the "4 km" sign. A sturdy log bridge crosses an active creek. Above it a waterfall comes down through a canyon off the north ridge of Mount Sproatt. You get a good look at it once you've crossed the bridge and climbed up the bank a short distance. If you're here on a summer's morning, position yourself with the sun shining down on you. Look up into the cedars to see backlit spider webs strung between the trees, arranged like a totem of dartboards, waiting for flies to hit the bull's-eye. Though the branches seem impossibly far apart for spiders to span, they perform like trapeze artists on the end of their silk threads. Moments like this are among the subtle little joys of the Rainbow Lake trail.

The trail climbs up and down for the next half-hour, with an occasional rare glimpse of 21-Mile Creek below. Once you've rounded Mount Sproatt, the trail levels as it crosses a wet meadow on a series of short boardwalks. Views of Rainbow Mountain begin to appear on your right. You can see now that, instead of one distinct peak, Rainbow Mountain has a series of crests. In warm months wild azaleas will be blooming in delicate shades of white beside the trail. (Just before the trail crosses Tonic Creek on a sturdy wooden plank bridge, two trails lead off to the left within a short distance of each other, a rough new one and an older one in better shape. Both go to Tonic Lake, an interesting side journey up an open valley, an hour from the boardwalk.)

The trail climbs steadily for another 30 minutes. Rainbow Lake seems to be tantalizingly close as you pass one kilometre marker and then another. You finally cross 21-Mile Creek over the biggest bridge on the whole trail, twice as large as any other you've seen. The creek is fed by many other, smaller tributaries before it achieves the volume to create the impressive waterfall near its conclusion.

The creek's exit point from Rainbow Lake is marked by a much smaller, though no less impressive, waterfall from Rainbow Lake. Climb up beside it and see how Rainbow Lake is naturally dammed at its east end, creating the waterfall. As your last steps bring you up to the top of the falls, the lake is suddenly laid out before you. The water near the shore is a clear golden hue, changing to turquoise as the depth increases. By now you'll be looking for a place to relax, perhaps even swim. There are several open campsites near the waterfall, and others at intervals as you follow the trail around the north side of the lake. The slope on the south side holds shelves of snow until well into the summer; some years it never completely melts.

I've heard it said that this lake is named Rainbow because of the trout that flourish in its waters. This may very well be true—certainly a number of hikers carry fishing rods in their backpacks. I also know that if you position yourself on a rock overlooking the lake so that you can see the sun reflecting on the lake bottom, rainbow patterns will occur. These are prismatic effects colouring the shadows cast by ripples on the lake's surface.

You may be content to rest awhile at lakeside and then head back down. Or you may meet a party coming the opposite way from Madeley Lake with whom you've arranged in advance to exchange car keys. (See the Callaghan Lake Road chapter for more information.) Or you may climb any of the ridges on either Rainbow or Sproatt mountains within an hour's range of the lake. Both of these mountains have open slopes with relatively easy footing. There is little that is concealed about their eroded peaks. It's just a question of having the time to reach them.

MOUNT SPROATT   From the ridges near the top of Mount Sproatt are great, intense views in all directions—as many peaks as you can possibly identify, congregated in one panoramic scene. You look down on several small lakes tucked into the folds of the ridges around Rainbow Lake. As you climb east along several ridges towards the top of Mount Sproatt you lose sight of Rainbow Lake but can now see Tonic Lake in the valley below. The meadows beside it have an open, inviting appearance. In the distance you can tell where the boardwalk trail runs. If you have several hours to spare, and good weather, you can find your way down off the ridge and back to the boardwalk without having to retrace your steps around Rainbow Lake. You'll have to remove your footwear to cross several creeks (you'll find the red heather underfoot surprisingly soft if you want to remain barefoot between crossings). Halfway down, watch for surveyor's tape and an occasional bike tread to show you the way. Stay in the open and you should be fine. There's no need to navigate any rock slides; just follow the natural lie of the land. Let the mountain lead you down from snow patches to the ridges below, which are moderately steep chutes carpeted with berry bushes and heather. Stay in the middle of the valley for most of the distance.

As you leave the ridge, views to the east of Wedge Mountain and the Blackcomb and Horstman glaciers give way to prominent Rainbow Mountain. The late afternoon sun begins to descend and cast a zigzag pattern of light and shade on Rainbow's glacier ice. Four bumpy peaks mark the mountain's brow. The only drawback can be the pesky presence of helicopters full of sightseers. Rainbow Lake must be on the flight

Snow can linger into midsummer on the ridges of Mount Sproatt.

plan. I'm sure the passengers look down on this scene of beauty and wish they could linger longer. Through your own efforts, you can take as long as you like!

You'll be tired but happy on the way back down along the main trail. Trees begin to increase in girth as you walk through an endless network of their roots. As you leave the forest behind, suddenly there are views of Blackcomb's runs; Iago, Fitzsimmons, and Overlord mountains; village rooftops and Alta Lake too, all at once. It's a release and a relief to feel the end is in sight. Head for Rainbow Park for a quick plunge to clean up. Alta Lake will feel a lot warmer once you've swum in Rainbow's waters.

17 | SINGING PASS TRAIL

CAMPING ◄
CYCLING ◄
HIKING ◄
VIEWPOINTS ◄

Fitzsimmons Creek flows west off the slopes of Overlord Mountain into Green Lake. The wide valley through which it makes its descent separates Whistler and Blackcomb mountains. Singing Pass stands in the headwaters region of Fitzsimmons Creek, 7.4 mi. (12 km) from Whistler Village. A road and trail leading to the pass run along the north side of Whistler Mountain, the slope originally intended for ski development in 1965. Outstanding mine claims on the Fitzsimmons side of Whistler Mountain forced a relocation of the proposed site to Whistler Creek on the mountain's west side. It took another 10 years before the claims were finally settled. Only then did the plan for Whistler Village and the Blackcomb ski facility begin taking shape.

Miners were some of the first Europeans to visit Whistler. Claims have been staked and holes dug throughout Whistler Valley for the past century. Harry Horstman was an early one, and Mount Sproatt was one of his favourites. Bill Bailiff was another old-timer. He ran a trap line in winter and in summer cleared trails around Cheakamus Lake and into Singing Pass.

VILLAGE TO GARIBALDI PARK   Singing Pass lies within Garibaldi Provincial Park, which was created by the government in 1920 through the lobbying efforts of local mountaineering groups. B.C. Parks has greatly upgraded the trail to Singing Pass since Bill Bailiff's time, but near the top of the pass you can still see his handiwork. (See Whistler Mountain chapter for map of this area.)

The road to Singing Pass begins from Whistler Village. B.C. Parks has signs indicating the turnoff to the trailhead on Highway 99 at both sets of lights where traffic turns into the village. Drive up Blackcomb Way as it approaches the bridge over Fitzsimmons Creek. Instead of crossing the creek, turn right at the sign indicating Singing Pass. This wide, paved section is also for buses to turn in.

From all appearances it looks as if you are supposed to begin driving straight up Whistler Mountain. For a short distance you do just that. Follow the dirt road uphill past the "Singing Pass 4.8 km" sign. Overhead is the Whistler Express. Quite soon you pass to the left of a gated private road leading up Whistler Ski Corporation property. (Guidelines for walkers wishing to follow this road are displayed on a large sign.)

The narrow road to the Singing Pass parking lot climbs relentlessly uphill. Views of the valley open before you. Use caution, and sound your horn at blind corners. (If you are cycling be prepared for a good throat-parching pump.) The parking lot has room for a dozen cars; if it's full, pull off tightly on the side of the road as close to the lot as you can get. The boundary of Garibaldi Provincial Park is 1.9 mi. (3 km) up the trail from the parking lot.

(Bicycles are not permitted in the park but you can ride as far as the boundary, which takes you past an old mine site and across a cooling stream. Also at the trailhead is an outhouse. A trail beside it descends to Fitzsimmons Creek. An old log bridge spans the creek. If it's passable, cross and then head back to the village via the Blackcomb service road, finishing the loop of your bike journey. For current conditions on this trail, known to Whistler cyclists as Little Spearhead, check with the staff at Jim McConkey's Sports Shop [932-2311] in the village. They run cycling tours of Whistler Mountain.)

The first 15-minute section of the Singing Pass Trail takes you over some of the steepest and roughest parts. Good footwear with upper-ankle support and a nonskid sole will make it easier to negotiate the loose surface. You will be crossing several creeks without bridges and may even encounter snow. If your shoes are waterproof, so much the better. Pace yourself, as you'll be on this trail for 3 hours. No need to burn out early.

Coming upon the mine shaft entrance is always a bit of a surprise. Old twisted tracks exit from a hole in the side of the mountain, dangling in space where a roadbed once was. Wooden beams support the entrance-way. A small stream trickles out. Darkness hides the interior of the shaft, which is partially blocked to keep casual explorers out. Beware low oxygen levels should you consider an in-depth appraisal. (After pumping uphill on the forest trail, cyclists may feel like the whole mountain-side is a low-oxygen zone.)

The trail varies from moderate to steep as it rises past Harmony Creek, which you'll have to pick your way across—there isn't a bridge. A short distance on, a bridge spans a smaller creek between the "2 km" and "3 km" signs. A constant wind coming down the slopes of Whistler Mountain blows a fine spray off the white water. All of Blackcomb's south face is showing across the valley now. This is the boundary of Garibaldi Park, as far as you can come by bicycle at present. The trail divides, with a sign pointing to the left for Singing Pass. The road on the right leads up Whistler Mountain to the base of the Blue chairlift.

SINGING PASS   A long, moderate, shaded section begins, leading past small and large creeks. An occasional bird call comes down through the forest from a junco or a woodpecker. The sound of Fitzsimmons Creek from the valley below is louder here. Shortly past the "3 km" sign, a good viewpoint to the north opens up in the forest where a violent windstorm in the winter of 1990-91 brought down a number of tall trees.

A sign announces Oboe Creek. The bridge over it is a good place to rest and watch the sun shining down through the canyon above, illuminating the white water. Moderate but steady climbing brings you to the "4 km" sign; 20 minutes beyond here the trail passes beside a large wooden arrow positioned on an old stump, pointing uphill. Bill Bailiff's old trail leads downhill towards Melody Creek, a pleasant but often wet walk. The newer trail continues on uphill. Looking down you can see the old trail where it passes through clearings in the forest. The forest begins to thin out as you gain altitude.

The new trail crosses Melody Creek at the "6 km" marker. You are entering the subalpine zone. After 2 hours in the shelter of the forest, it's a relief to reach an open area. The walking for the past 30 minutes has been easy and continues to be so. Above you, the open slopes may hold snow as late as August. Fitzsimmons Creek is out of earshot now, as the trail has been leading away from it, towards Singing Pass.

(Past the "7 km" marker watch for a trail resembling a small creekbed leading uphill off the main path. This is the turnoff for the Musical Bumps trail leading west across Oboe, Flute and Piccolo summits. It's still another hour before you reach the halfway point on this rocky trail to Harmony Lake and the Roundhouse where the Whistler Express arrives.)

You will know that you are close to Singing Pass when flowers begin appearing beside the trail. From June to August the slopes are alive with colourful blossoms. Glacier lilies begin blooming in June, followed by white Sitka valerian, yellow fan-leaf cinqefoil, orange Indian paintbrush, tall yellow western pasque flowers, and blue lupines. Most years flowers will be in full bloom by the first weekend in August, lasting several weeks. Years when the snowmelt is slower the flowering may be delayed until mid-August. An interpretive sign positioned beside the trail lets you know that you've reached the pass.

Two small ponds appear on your left as you reach the pass, perfect for soaking tired feet while enjoying the views to the west. Don't resist the chance to climb just a little higher past this point even though the trail does begin to incline steeply towards an open ridge. The best views are only another 10 to 15 minutes beyond the pass. With each step you

Wildflowers bloom in profusion every August in Singing Pass.

take, more peaks, glaciers, and even turquoise Cheakamus Lake come into view until you are seeing Garibaldi park in the round. Small groves of alpine fir offer shelter from the breeze, which can blow cool even on the hottest days. When you see the glaciers holding the surrounding peaks in their grip, you understand why the wind coming off the slopes isn't warmer. You would do well to take a lightweight windbreaker with you, even on days when it's hot in the valley.

In the 1950s, the sound of the wind blowing across the slopes here inspired Ottar Brandvold to christen this Singing Pass while on a camping trip with his wife, Joan Matthews, and his brother Emil, owners of the Diamond Head Chalet.

RUSSET LAKE   People who come this far with intentions of camping overnight must carry on to Russet Lake, another half-hour beyond the ridge above Singing Pass. If snow conditions or weariness weigh you down, rest in the sheltered grove at Singing Pass to the left of a sign asking hikers to be careful when walking on the delicate alpine undergrowth. A rough trail leads to a number of clearings in the grove, with beautiful views to the west of Rainbow Mountain.

The 1.2-mi. (2-km) trail from Singing Pass to Russet Lake is marked by rock cairns. Even if there is still snow you can find your way to the ridge above the lake by following these markers. You may wonder about the occasional red patches on the snow, which look as if they have been

Russet Lake lies at the foot of Fissile Peak.

coloured with dye. These are colonies of algae that grow in summer months.

Rising above Russet Lake are the crumbling red slopes of Fissile Peak. It stands in the way of Overlord Mountain, blocking views of the predominant peak at the east end of the Fitzsimmons Valley. Once you have gotten your bearings, you will be able to distinguish parts of Overlord as they appear to the east of Fissile Peak. Farther east is the Cheakamus Glacier, veined with crevasses, on the slopes of Mount Davidson. Beside it, Castle Towers Creek flows through a wide valley into Cheakamus Lake. (The sounds of this creek are audible from the Singing Creek campsite at lakeside.) Nonetheless, you must climb Singing Pass in order to get a true appreciation for the scope of the valley. B.C. Parks plans to cut a trail from Cheakamus Lake to Singing Pass in the future.

Once you've reached the ridge above Singing Pass, you'll see a red roof beside Russet Lake's north end. The Alpine Club of Canada built this cabin, large enough to hold eight climbers. In good weather, tents sprout around the perimeter of the lake. As well as climbers, this area attracts many visitors who come to see the abundant floral display.

Groves of alpine fir dot the slopes. Their distinctive black cones stand straight up, fat as your thumb. Deer or mountain goats shelter in these groves: you'll see the smooth beds they have fashioned for themselves, and smell their strong, musky scent. They nibble on the interior branches of the conifers, leaving the outside limbs full for protection.

RETURN TRIP   You have more time to look around on your way back down. Birds feed in the heather and in the branches of the sturdy western hemlock. They don't seem to be shy of onlookers. Groups of fat ptarmigan launch themselves off rock outcrops, showing a great expanse of wing with impressive feathering. They moult three times a year, changing camouflage to match the seasons. Beware the grey jays called whisky-jacks, who will steal your lunch if it's left unguarded.

Looking out across the meadow below the pond at Singing Pass you will see Bill Bailiff's old trail winding downward. It links with the new trail farther down beside the large wooden arrow. The two trails are never far apart; the old one grows faint near the arrow junction, but the old notched logs crossing some of the wet areas remain. There is some magnificent old-growth along the worn trail. One blow-down near Melody Creek must be the biggest tree to have grown on this mountain in the last thousand years.

The wide new trail is so easy to follow that you may wish to remain at Singing Pass during the "magic hour" before sunset, then walk back down in the afterglow.

Note: Occasionally heavy rains trigger a landslide on the road to the parking lot at Singing Pass, making it impassable. Until an alternative route is cleared, the only approach to Singing Pass is via the Musical Bumps trail from the top of Whistler Mountain. To check on the current condition of the Singing Pass road, call B.C. Parks in Squamish at 898-3678.

18 | GREEN LAKE HYDRO TRAIL TO PARKHURST

CYCLING ◄
PADDLING ◄
WALKING ◄

Of the five principal lakes in the Whistler Valley, Green Lake is the largest and most challenging. Together the other four—Alpha, Nita, Alta and Lost Lake—would easily fit within its confines. Green Lake is also sparsely populated and therefore a prime location for recreational exploration. There are only a few dozen homes at Emerald Estates on the lake's northwest corner. Just across the lake from Emerald Estates is the ghost town of Parkhurst.

There are a limited number of access points to Green Lake: from the Valley trail at the lake's south end, from Green Lake Park at the north end, or from the hydro road running along the lake's east side. (See Valley Trail chapter for map of this area).

HYDRO ROAD   You really have to make your mind up to do this road. It's close to Whistler Village but remote at the same time. And there's not much sense in doing only half of it. Once you've reached the opposite end of Green Lake you won't want to retrace your steps. This requires planning. I suggest making a 14-mi. (23-km) round-trip of it, linking with Highway 99. Otherwise, arrange to be picked up or dropped off at the Wedgemount parking lot. (By bike, Green Lake's east side is a test. You'll be surprised at how good you feel once you've accomplished it. And it will prepare you for even longer rides.)

To reach the rough road that runs along the east side of Green Lake, follow the Valley trail north from the village past Lost Lake to the open hillside above Fitzsimmons Creek. Instead of following the Valley trail down to Green Lake, take the rough road that leads north beside the hydro towers. There are trail markers at this junction.

The rough road climbs steadily higher above the lake with two good viewpoints where it momentarily levels off. From here you look west across Green Lake to Highway 99 on the opposite shore and the roofs of the Alpine Meadows neighbourhood on the lower slopes of Rainbow

The truck that put the "park" in Parkhurst.

Mountain. The first quarter of the way up the lake is the toughest. If you are cycling you just have to settle in and pump hard. Otherwise, dismount and push your way on some of the steeper stretches. If you are walking, wear sturdy shoes, as this section of the road is surfaced with loose gravel.

Just when it looks as if the road will climb even higher towards the hydro tower up on the cliff face, it levels and begins to descend and then rises again through old-growth forest. The best part of the walk or ride is from here north to the Wedgemount Lake parking lot. The sandy surface of the road is easier to handle than the rocks and loose gravel on the south end. There is a fun downhill section of the road leading to Wedge Creek where you can release your brakes and just let your bike fly. This is also one of the prettiest sections.

The road finally meets the B.C. Rail tracks, 45 minutes by bike from Green Lake's south end. Follow the tracks over the bridge where Wedge Creek flows into the Green River, to where a trail leads off on the right to a gravel pit and service road. From this point there is yet another good downhill stretch where you can safely let the bike run at its own speed down to the river. The road goes on farther to Rethel Creek from here and there's not much to see. Instead, I recommend taking the short trail beside the Green River to the railway bridge that leads across to the Wedgemount parking lot beside Highway 99. A large red metal gate stands beside the parking lot where a logging bridge over the Green River is located.

By bike, it's best to do the hydro road from south to north. This enables you to get the gravel out of the way going uphill rather than having to cope with it going down. It also allows you to enjoy the downhill runs at Green Lake's north end.

If you're walking, it's easier to go north to south, beginning from the Wedgemount Lake parking lot. This is also the shorter route to the ghost town of Parkhurst.

PARKHURST   As the hydro road nears the lake's north end, a side road leads off to the old mill town of Parkhurst. Watch for it as a sandy-surfaced, hilly section of the hydro road passes under the power lines, dropping down one side and rising again on the other, quite distinct from the rest of the road. As it's the only side road leading off towards Green Lake it won't be difficult to find, especially as there is an orange tape tied to one of the scrub alder marking the way. From here it is mostly downhill to lakeside, a 10-minute walk.

Parkhurst is hidden from view on the hillside above the east side of Green Lake. From Green Lake Park you can just make out an ancient yellow piece of heavy equipment akilter next to the B.C. Rail tracks. There is a little old dock in front of it where you can tie up if you boat over. Pilings from the original dock on the north side of this small point of land are still visible.

Exploring what remains of the mill town is one of the most interesting ways to discover traces of Whistler's past. Parkhurst was a prosperous place in its time, shipping more wood than any other mill along the B.C. Rail line in the Whistler Valley in the 1930s and '40s.

Florence Petersen, longtime Whistler resident and director of the Whistler Museum, recalls that after the mill closed a caretaker stayed on in the 1950s. Walking out to visit him was a Sunday pastime for residents of Alta Lake. Parkhurst enjoyed something of a revival as Hippietown in the 1960s. At present there are two houses occupied, one with a well-developed garden and a small barn. Several abandoned cars and trucks of assorted vintages are permanently parked beside the buildings that remain, some buried to their axles. Old stove pieces litter the ground. Privies and bunkhouses have been flattened after years of neglect and the weight of winter snow. The wood in some of the buildings is surprisingly fresh where it has recently been exposed after being covered by exterior walls for decades.

The millworkers' ramshackle residences are located on a ridge above the lake with the railway tracks running below. Several small, sturdy root cellars are built into the banks of the ridge beside the tracks. These predate the settlement of Parkhurst, and may have been food caches for prospectors who would be dropped off here on the way to their claims. They are similar to the small cabin (Jacquie's Place) on the hillside above the B.C. Rail tracks farther north and the rustic trapper's cabin on display at the Pemberton Museum.

19 | COUGAR MOUNTAIN AND ANCIENT CEDAR FOREST

CYCLING ◄
FISHING ◄
HIKING ◄
PADDLING ◄
PICNICKING ◄
SNOWMOBILING ◄
SNOWSHOEING ◄
WALKING ◄
X-C SKIING ◄

Logging in the Whistler Valley has fuelled the local economy for the past 70 years. Old photographs show that during summer months Alta and Green lakes were choked with log booms during the height of mill operations. Judging from what you see when you walk through nearby Garibaldi Provincial Park, where logging was restricted, the old-growth forest must have been magnificent when it covered the whole valley.

All is not lost. It is possible to visit an ancient stand of trees on Crown land that has survived the cut. As if to heighten the contrast and increase your appreciation for the magnificence of the ancient cedars on Cougar Mountain, the logging on the adjacent land is some of the most thorough anywhere.

16-MILE CREEK   The road to Cougar Mountain begins at the north end of Green Lake, 0.6 mi. (1 km) past the entrance to Emerald Estates. Take the two-lane gravel road that rises uphill on the left (west) side of Highway 99. A short way in you pass a brown Forest Service sign marking the beginning of the road along 16-Mile Creek. 16-Mile Creek flows into the Green River just north of the turnoff from Highway 99. Its headwaters are two small lakes south of the the Showh Lakes.

Just past the Forest Service sign there is a widening on the right (north) side of the road where snowmobilers, snowshoers, and cross-country skiers park in winter. Snow is not cleared past this point. If you wish to do the entire 12.4-mi. (20-km) journey by bicycle or on foot in summer, you can leave your vehicle here, or you can drive halfway to Cougar Mountain (beyond the halfway point are ditches that may be too deep for the average car to negotiate). Nearby are several buildings on the north side of the road, the winter location of Whistler Snowmobile Guided Tours (phone 932-4086). Proceed past them, ignoring the road branching off to the left (it leads along the recently logged south side of 16-Mile Creek).

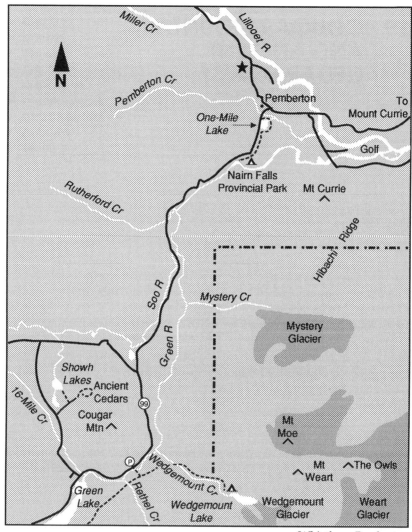

Whistler—Pemberton

For the first 2.5 mi. (4 km) the road proceeds along a level part of this small valley with the creek on its right side. There are some pleasant cedar trees overhanging small fishing holes along the way. Although the trees are a good size, they will seem like babies after you've seen Cougar Mountain.

A log bridge spans 16-Mile Creek, from which point the road begins to climb a ridge above the creek on the valley's north side. Beside the bridge is another good place to leave your car; from here on the road is often rutted by run-off. The ditches offer added excitement when you're

The Ancient Cedar Forest dwarfs everything—and everyone—else. (Randy Stoltmann)

going downhill on a bike. From the bridge to the Showh Lakes is 1.9 mi. (3 km), an easy hour's walk. Take something to drink when you set out on a warm day; there is no water until you reach the lakes.

SHOWH LAKES   Just before the lakes the road divides. (If you continue on to the left towards a ridge that has been cleared of trees, you will pass beside the smaller of the Showh Lakes. There is no easy access from the road to the lake. Beyond here this road becomes rougher as it heads north towards the Soo River logging road. For cyclists it's possible to link up with the Soo road, making a circle route back to Highway 99.) The road to Cougar Mountain heads uphill on the right. For the best access to the Showh Lakes, take this road. It continues uphill for 1.2 mi. (2 km). The larger of the two lakes appears below you halfway along. Watch for the trail to its shoreline on your left, leading down through stumps and blueberry bushes. If you've driven in with a boat, you can launch here. A good place to picnic is on top of a giant log half-submerged in the shallow water.

ANCIENT CEDARS LOOP TRAIL   The road climbs to its end 0.6 mi. (1 km) past the larger of the Showh Lakes. The 2.5-mi. (4-km) Ancient Cedars loop trail begins here. After the open light along the whole of the 16-Mile Creek road, the forest seems quite shadowy. White pigeon berries and the red fruits of devil's club stand out vividly among the evergreens by late August. (Beware the rhubarb-like leaves and spiny stems of devil's club, which can leave you with painful inflamed scratches.) Bike riders, hang on: this is a rocky, root-filled trail, soft in spots from years of cedar needles accumulating on the forest floor.

A small wooden bridge spans a creek beside a waterfall near the outset of the loop trail. Since this trail leads to some big trees, you begin to examine each one that you pass, sizing it up against your expectations. You can tell when you've found the ancient cedars: trunk sizes suddenly swell to 9 ft. (3 m) in diameter. On a hot day the shade they cast causes the temperature in this part of the forest to drop another degree.

Several enormous cedars sprout sideways to each other from a common base. Nearby, two giant blowdowns lie at 180 degrees to each other. Fungi climb the trunk of one cedar like a spiral staircase. Their orange flesh provides a rare splash of brightness.

As you slowly circle through the forest, it's hard not to wonder about the stumps around the larger of the Showh Lakes and the giant log where you picnicked. What is here in the grove of ancient cedars must have been elsewhere too. After the hush among these giants, it's refreshing to return to the bridge and just let the sound of the waterfall do your thinking for you for a while.

20 | WEDGEMOUNT LAKE

Of the five trails leading into Garibaldi Provincial Park from the Squamish-Whistler corridor, the one to Wedgemount Lake is the most formidable and least travelled. It's also one of the oldest. Harry Horstman blazed the original trail up the narrow canyon between Wedge and Weart mountains through which Wedgemount Creek drops into the Green River. He spent many summers prospecting around Wedgemount Lake, a turquoise gem set between Wedge Mountain, at 9540 ft. (2891 m) the highest peak in the park, and its neighbour to the north, Mount Weart. (While Wedge Mountain was named for its distinctive shape, Mount Weart memorializes the first chairman of the Garibaldi Parks Board.)

A short, wiry prospector with a bushy beard, Harry became friends with Myrtle and Alex Philip soon after they arrived at Alta Lake. One autumn in the early 1920s, Myrtle and Alex took two guests on a hike to Wedgemount to visit Harry. His remark on meeting them at the lake was that the new sport of hiking must be catching on, as they were the second group he'd seen since the beginning of the summer!

Today, the guest book in the little climber's cabin that stands beside Wedgemount Lake holds the comments of as many guests in a season as Horstman saw there in his lifetime. (Harry was still going strong when ski operations started at Whistler in the mid-1960s.) Some of the entries in the book are positively hair-raising. Here's a typical one from a recent January:

> Climbed through deep snow for six hours, minus 20 and blowing; ended up on the wrong side of the lake; thought we'd have to bivy in a snowbank for the night but with 15 minutes of daylight left we spotted the top of the privy sticking up above a drift; feels great to be here even though the cabin was half-full of snow that had drifted in through cracks in the door; the floor is like a skating rink because the

133

roof has been leaking again, but with a little effort we made it cozy and slept for 12 hours straight; never had such a great time in my life.

You'll feel that way too, even if you arrive with the sun shining in the middle of summer. The setting for this lake is unrivalled: a wide swath of glacier ice rising at the lake's east end, a panorama of peaks, wildflowers in bloom, a million stars overhead at night, clear air, and an immense silence.

Part of the release you experience when you arrive at Wedgemount Lake comes when you give yourself up to fatigue once you've made it. There are very few steps along the way that don't go one above the other. If you are just going up for the day with a light pack, it will take you between 2½ and 3½ hours. If you are carrying enough equipment to spend the night, add another 1 or 2 hours to cover the 5 mi. (8 km) from the parking lot to the lake. The total elevation gain is 3960 ft. (1200 m).

You begin from the parking lot beside Highway 99, 2.5 mi. (4 km) north of Emerald Estates. Use the logging bridge or cross the Green River on the B.C. Rail bridge. (See Cougar Mountain chapter for map of this area.) Check for oncoming trains before starting out, and be quick about crossing—there is no room on the short span to stand aside, and the Green River flowing below is deep and fast. Once across, follow the narrow trail beside the river to an open road. Turn left and walk the first 1.9 mi. (3 km) on a road of packed dirt and rocky creekbed. There are signs at each divide pointing the way to the lake. Alder line the way as the road rises through reforested slopes.

The road ends and the trail begins beside a large arrow outlined in stone pointing prophetically uphill. The rough trail climbs towards Wedgemount Creek, crossing it on a log bridge. One of the larger trees on the trail stands directly above the bridge. Round it towards another bridge crossing a smaller stream. Except for glimpses of Wedgemount Creek higher up the mountain, this is the last water you'll find until you reach the foot of an avalanche slope, about 2 hours away.

Now it's just a question of climbing. The trail leads through the shelter of the old-growth forest. At first the canopy of branches is so thick that very little below can compete for light. The forest floor is open and mossy. Soon the girth of the conifers begins to dwindle and smaller trunks provide handholds for you to lift and push yourself forward. Wild azaleas rush to put out blossoms in the short growing season. The trail is a constant series of switchbacks that take you away from the creek, then bring you back within a short distance of it as it drops straight down through a canyon worn bare by its action. You'll have to leave the main trail for a better look at it, but this requires only a few steps downhill to a viewing point.

The tongue of the Wedgemount Glacier licks the shore of this small alpine lake. (Randy Stoltmann)

After crossing a short stretch of scree at the foot of an old slide that must have occurred several centuries ago, the trail enters its final, steepest stage. This is the most difficult part, not only because of the elevation gained with every step, but also because in late spring and early summer the path doubles as a creekbed. In contrast to the other four park trails, there are very few markers along the Wedgemount route. There is no indication that you are nearing the top until you have almost arrived. Watch for the number "7" affixed high on the trunk of an alpine fir, a sign that the end is near. A short distance above here is the small cabin with room for six around its two tables and in the narrow loft. The outhouse is most distinctive, a bullet-shaped, metal-clad model that looks poised for liftoff.

You'll have to clamber down a rocky slope to reach the lake. The ice of the Wedgemount Glacier reaches down to the shore of the lake's east end. Now that you've made it, you have all the time you want to enjoy yourself—unless, of course, the weather turns cold, robbing you of precious body heat. Perspiration will have soaked through much of your clothing by the time you reach the lake. If you're wearing cotton, remember that it leaches heat out of your body 200 times faster than it can be replaced. Beware the debilitating effects of hypothermia. For protection pack along an extra layer or two of warm, waterproof clothing in case of a shift in the weather. Remember, you'll need all of your remaining strength for the descent, which is even trickier in the first stages than the climb up. Even in dry weather the trail can be slippery.

By the time you reach the parking lot again, you'll be happy to dry off and head down to Whistler for some refreshment. Be sure to toast Harry's memory when you do.

PEMBERTON |

MEANDERING RIVERS AND
MOUNTAIN MEADOWS

The Lillooet River Valley is a broad flood plain built up in a trench carved by glaciers, the last of which remain on the slopes of Mount Meager in the valley's northern region. The fertile meadows of the Pemberton area are composed of layer upon layer of sediment, carried down from the slopes each spring during run-off, which has covered the debris left by the glacier to a depth of a mile (1.6 km).

The Lillooet River originally meandered back and forth across the valley floor, frequently overflowing its banks following run-off and heavy rain. After decades of lobbying the B.C. government for action, capped by a particularly damaging flood in 1940, a program was begun to regulate the river's flow. For flood control, much of the swampland in the upper river valley was drained, and the course of the river was changed by a network of dikes and ditches. Now it flows in a much straighter line and as a result moves much more quickly. This has sped up the erosion of the riverbanks; silt carried down to the northern end of Lillooet Lake has filled in more than a mile (1.6 km) of wetland in the past hundred years. Another consequence of the diking is that farmers can no longer rely on flooding to fertilize their fields with rich silt. Artificial soil enrichment has been adopted. A flood occurred in August 1991 such as is forecast to occur only once or twice a century, breaching the dike in several places.

The Royal Engineers arrived in the area in the 1850s, and chief surveyor Lieutenant Palmer named a small port at the north end of Lillooet Lake in honour of Joseph Pemberton, the surveyor-general of Vancouver Island. Miners gave the name Pemberton (or Lillooet) Meadows to the region as they passed through towards Anderson Lake on the Douglas Trail (also known as the Gold Rush Trail). Today Pemberton Meadows refers to the area settled in the upper valley region, north of the bridge over the Ryan River (which itself has moved up in the cartographic world; in earlier times it was simply known as Ryan Creek).

The Coast Mountains running to the northwest cast long shadows into the valley, affecting winter temperatures. The moderating influence of coastal storms does not penetrate here, resulting in much colder conditions than in Whistler or even the higher elevations near D'Arcy. Weather records show that once in a decade the bottom drops out of the thermometer in Pemberton. In 1949, for example, several weeks of extremely low temperatures—in the -40°C range—kept everyone indoors except to perform the most essential chores. This was repeated most recently in the winter of 1989/90. Less than half the year is frost-free, and frost can arrive as early as August in some parts of the valley.

Winter snow conditions can be fickle, ranging from 6 inches to 6 feet (15 cm to 1.8 m) in January depending on the year. Statistics can be somewhat misleading when a year such as 1972 is taken into account: 30 ft. (9 m) of snow fell that season. Annual precipitation averages 40 in. (100 cm) during the winter months. In summer the average rainfall is only 7 in. (18 cm), which is terrific for recreation but makes irrigation essential for farming.

In the 1920s and 1930s many Pemberton farmers worked together to achieve pest-free status for the valley's potatoes. In this way they were able to develop an international market for their disease-free seed crop. The area farmers were so successful at growing potatoes that in the 1930s Pemberton won first prize at the Chicago International Fair five years running. (Growers in other parts of the continent became so discouraged that Pemberton was asked to withdraw from the competition for several years to give someone else a chance.) If you're visiting the area in September, you might like to taste some of these fine potatoes: you'll find many farms in the area advertising produce for sale. In early fall you can sometimes also buy pine mushrooms, picked in the surrounding forests and sold at high prices to buyers seeking this prized delicacy for Asian markets.

21 | WHISTLER-
PEMBERTON
ROAD

CAMPING ◄
CYCLING ◄
DRIVING ◄
FISHING ◄
PICNICKING ◄
SWIMMING ◄
VIEWPOINTS ◄
WALKING ◄

When Highway 99 was finally pushed through from Squamish to Whistler in 1964, the citizens of Pemberton expected that it would soon link up with their town. The farmers in the valley 22 mi. (35 km) north of Whistler had lobbied for years for improved access to the coast, after relying on the railroad for the better part of the century. Like most improvements between Pemberton and the outside world, the extension of Highway 99 north to their town did not come as easily or as quickly as they would have liked, but it finally arrived in the mid-'70s. Improvements in the early 1980s made this section of the highway the most enjoyable of all to drive. It is smooth-surfaced, well-banked, with frequent passing lanes, making the 30-minute trip a pleasure.

There are many interesting geographical features along the way between Whistler and Pemberton. Linking the two towns is the Green River, flowing north into the Lillooet River. Two important tributaries, the Soo River and Rutherford Creek, feed the Green along the way. There is a stunningly powerful waterfall, Nairn Falls, on the Green River at the neck of the valley just before the outskirts of Pemberton. Much of this you can see while looking out the window of your car as you motor along. (See Valley Trail and Cougar Mountain chapters for maps of this area.)

But for the best look at these roadside delights, nothing beats making this journey by bicycle. A large part of the reason for this is the attention that the highway builders have paid to the creation of wide shoulders, especially designed with cyclists in mind. The only exception is the section of road close to Nairn Falls at the northern end of the Whistler Valley, where riders must be extremely careful for a short distance.

The round-trip journey takes about 4 hours, but you may complete it in more or less time, depending on your bike, your physical condition and whether you decide to include some of the off-road sights. On the

The Green River accompanies the highway on most of its journey from Whistler to Pemberton.

way north there is one mighty steep hill and several long, thrilling descents, making it the easier of the two legs. If you are planning to do the complete circuit, be sure to save enough energy for several extended hill-climbs on the way south. During warmer months you will have plenty of company along the way; many of the Whistler workers who live in Pemberton commute by bicycle.

Weekends are always a better time to attempt this ride, as there are fewer commercial trucks on the road then. The wash from logging trucks is more of a concern on the southbound side of the road as they are fully loaded in this lane; you will rarely, if ever, see logs being trucked north.

GREEN LAKE—WEST SIDE   The Valley trail crosses Highway 99 at the bridge over the River of Golden Dreams. This is a good place to link up with the highway. A short distance north of this crossing Highway 99 passes beside the entrance to the Alpine Meadows neighbourhood. The wide shoulders are paved from this point north; from here to Whistler's most northerly neighbourhood, Emerald Estates, they form part of the Valley trail system.

As you ride over the bridge that spans 19-Mile Creek you will notice a rough side road leading down alongside the creek (it's suitable for bicycles only for a short distance before it turns into a winding walking trail leading towards the creek mouth on Green Lake). Highway 99 swings away from Green Lake for a short distance at this point in order to skirt the marshy delta where the creek enters the lake.

The highway rises gently past Whistler Fire Hall No. 2 and then an old quarry where there are now several businesses, including the Whistler Helicopter Service. This was the site of the old Rainbow Tow, a small ski area that operated from the late 1960s to the 1970s. In its heyday it was quite popular with Whistler residents because it used to be lit for night skiing.

Just past the quarry the highway swings back beside Green Lake. There is a pull-out here with two colourful interpretive signs, put up by the Resort Municipality of Whistler, that will help you identify wildlife and the profile of the peaks that rise on the east side of the lake. This is an excellent spot for photographs of the east side of the valley. The banks of the lake drop off steeply; there won't be an opportunity to get down beside the water until you reach the entrance to Emerald Estates, a short distance north of here.

At Emerald there are three points of public access to the lake, all of them good places to take a break from the highway. At the south end of Summer Lane is a small, rough approach to the lake, not visible from the highway. At the north end of the lane is a formal boat launch, complete with dock and picnic area. You can see this as you are driving by. The most pleasant of the three access points is Green Lake Park. Just before the boat launch watch for Lakeshore Drive; follow it around a short distance to Green Lake Park. There is room for six cars to park here. The park consists of a treed area, a small beach, five picnic tables (two with barbecues), and an outhouse. There are good views to the south of Whistler Mountain.

Green Lake narrows at its north end, where the Green River begins. As you ride north you get a very real sense of how the grade of the valley declines gradually towards Pemberton, encouraging the flow of the Green River in that direction.

GREEN RIVER CROSSING   North of Emerald the road follows beside the lake for a short distance and passes the turnoff to Cougar Mountain on the highway's west side. Down through the trees you can now see the Green River. From this point on the river will be a frequent companion, accessible at a variety of locations when refreshment is required. The highway crosses over 16-Mile Creek, which runs under the road through a culvert just before it joins the river. (The parking lot at the Wedgemount Lake trailhead is several bends in the highway past here. Access to the east side of the river is the BCR bridge to the right of the parking lot. For more on this trail, see the Green Lake Hydro Trail and Wedgemount Lake chapters.) At this point you are 7.4 miles (12 km) north of Whistler Village.

As the highway climbs north from here, it passes the large wooden sign that marks the boundary of the Resort Municipality of Whistler. Settle into your ride and carry on up a gentle incline. The river falls away from view now; it won't rejoin the highway for 6 mi. (10 km). The grade of the land carries the river to the east side of the valley while Highway 99 stays to the west.

The forest on each side of the highway has been logged for the next 6 mi. (10 km). While the second-growth is beginning to rise again gradually, there is little shelter from rainstorms or the broiling sun along this section. The road climbs moderately, then begins a long, gradual descent. Leading off to the west is the Soo River logging road. It heads west, eventually meeting the 16-Mile Creek road and forming a loop around Cougar Mountain.

Where the highway descends to meet the BCR tracks at a spot known as Green River Crossing, there is a tiny cabin on the south bank of the steep hillside above the tracks, a short distance west of the highway. Even if you're not seeking shelter this may be a good place to take a break, as you will have taken at least 30 minutes to reach this point from Whistler by bike. Time to give those muscles a rest.

While the tiny cabin's history isn't known, it is so sturdily built that though it long ago outlived its original purpose it survives relatively intact. Its chunky timbers are 12 in. (30 cm) thick and 18 in. (45 cm) wide; there are three or four timbers to a wall—not quite big enough to sleep in but cozy nevertheless. The peaked roof is showing the most wear, but the interior is still surprisingly snug and clean. From the doorway is a good view of Mount Weart and north to Mount Currie. Someone has painted "Jacquie's Place—Girls Only" on the front of the cabin, but don't let that stop you. The password here is "Any port in a storm."

A short distance farther west down the tracks from Jacquie's Place is a small lake that can also be seen from the highway as you head north beyond the railway crossing. If you walk the tracks past the lake you will soon come to a railway bridge over the Soo River with a good view of the canyon. This isn't visible from the highway, so it is worth the detour. There is plenty of clearance on each side of the tracks so there is no need to be overly apprehensive of approaching trains. (In fact, I always hope one will come along but this seldom happens.) A trail leads down to the Soo River from the north side of the bridge. Tall cottonwoods and poplars overhang the river. When water levels are low broad sandbars appear, ideal for fishermen and picnickers.

Back on Highway 99 just past the Green River railway crossing, a gravel road leads off to the west past a weigh-station. This road leads to two quarries. It is actively used by large trucks during the week, but on weekends you can ride through the first quarry that you come to on a road that runs down and across the Green River. There really isn't much of interest on the river here, but as the road is not steep you may wish to ride down for a look anyway.

SOO RIVER TO RUTHERFORD CREEK   As you continue north the highway descends through a series of bends in the road with the Soo River canyon below on the west. This is an enjoyable section (try not to dwell on the thought that on the return journey it will all be uphill). You will be sailing along by the time the highway levels out.

The Soo River now runs level with the highway for a short way before it joins the Green River. There is a pull-out beside the highway on the bank of the Soo just before the bridge that carries you across. This is a good fishing spot; there are also several rough campsites in the forest beside the river. A short distance farther north, on each side of the Soo River bridge, are signs of the old highway. The bridge is 3.7 miles (6 km) north of Jacquie's Place. Just after you cross the bridge watch for a small road leading down to the river on the east side of the highway. This is another good spot for fishing.

It's a mile and a bit (2 km) between the Soo River and Rutherford Creek bridges. Along the way there is a series of small side roads leading off to the east. Most of them are B.C. Hydro service roads. A local Boy Scout troop has planted sections of the Hydro right of way with Christmas trees.

There are old roads on both sides of the Rutherford Creek bridge, leading to the creek itself or to lookouts on the banks above the creek. On the west side of the highway a road leads through a large quarry to logging sites along Rutherford Creek. Someday this may be a pretty sight, but at present it's one that makes me avert my eyes. Echo Lake, a half-hour climb along the badly eroded logging road on Rutherford Creek's south side, has been shamefully treated by loggers, who have

If you cycle Highway 99 between Whistler and Pemberton, you'll appreciate a dip in warm One-Mile Lake, just before Pemberton.

removed all of the tree cover at lakeside. Although there may be fish in Echo Lake, it hardly seems worth the effort to get there.

NAIRN FALLS-PEMBERTON   The highway north of Rutherford Creek is level for 1.2 mi. (2 km) with the Green River once more on its east side. There are some good picnic spots beside the river; if you're heading north, this may be a good place to rest before you tackle the steepest climb on the trip. Highway 99 runs underneath a B.C. Rail overpass, then climbs steadily through a series of switchbacks for almost 2 mi. (3 km). This is a very difficult passage, especially because the highway shoulder is extremely narrow in places. The Green River now squeezes through a canyon below the road just before it plunges over Nairn Falls. Once you've reached the crest of the hill, it's a gentle coast down to the entrance of Nairn Falls Provincial Park.

Highway 99 continues its downhill run for another mile (1.6 km) to One-Mile Lake. The water in this small lake is warm. A boardwalk now runs around the shoreline, allowing wheelchair and buggy access. A trail links the lake with nearby Nairn Falls park. (See the chapter on Nairn Falls for a further description.)

You have now reached Pemberton. Having made your way through the narrow canyon at the north end of the Whistler valley, it's a release to see the Pemberton Valley open up before you. There's a special feeling to this valley, with its cleared fields and wide views of the surrounding mountains. A choice of further directions for exploration presents itself when Highway 99 reaches its end. If you've just cycled the 22 mi. (35 km) one-way from Whistler you're probably feeling a bit saddle-sore and in need of refreshment. The historic Pemberton Hotel is a short distance away. You can quench your thirst here before making the return trip or heading off around the valley for more adventures. If you've had enough for one day, you can always ride the bus back. Maverick Coach Lines is located two blocks from the hotel on Aster Street, opposite the municipal office. (For a better rate, ask the driver to ship your bike as freight. Chances are good that it will be on the same bus as you. It will be dropped off in Whistler at the freight office at Nesters shopping plaza.) Once you've had a chance to ride this road, it won't seem as long or as steep again.

22 | NAIRN FALLS PROVINCIAL PARK

BIRD-WATCHING ◄
CAMPING ◄
CYCLING ◄
FISHING ◄
HIKING ◄
PICNICKING ◄
SWIMMING ◄
VIEWPOINTS ◄
WALKING ◄

As the Green River nears Pemberton it increases considerably in volume, picking up water from the Soo River and Rutherford Creek. Suddenly its broad shape is transformed into a thundering column of whitewater as it drops 200 ft. (60 m) at Nairn Falls. Almost as quickly as the drama began, the river resumes its former character and courses on towards Lillooet Lake.

The neck of the Whistler Valley, where this transformation occurs, is also the route through which the railway, Highway 99, and a string of B.C. Hydro towers squeeze themselves. It's a powerful place to visit. The air is filled with mist, the ground shakes, the bald rock face on which you stand seems linked directly to the earth's core. Tall trees cover the slopes of Mount Currie, rising steeply from the canyon floor. From down here you can't see the peaks of its broad comb, but several will come into view as you walk the trail from the nearby provincial park.

A bridge once crossed the top of Nairn Falls (called Green River Falls on older maps). One pioneer recalls that walking across seemed to bring you face-to-face with your own mortality, a sense heightened by first having to walk along the railway tracks to reach the bridge. Do not use the railway approach.

The better part of the apprehension associated with visiting the falls was done away with in 1966 when the provincial park was created here. Until Highway 99 connected Pemberton with Whistler several years later, the park was enjoyed solely by residents and visitors who arrived in the Pemberton Valley by rail. (See Cougar Mountain chapter for map of this area.)

The new approach to the falls is a main feature of the park. It begins from the visitor parking lot just inside the park gates off Highway 99, 1.9 mi. (3 km) south of Pemberton. The trail to Nairn Falls is not long, only 1.1 mi. (1.8 km). You pass along a ridge, high above the green waters of the river at first. (Do not attempt this when conditions are icy.) Parents with young children should walk cautiously on this narrow path. The embankment drops away sharply as the trail cuts through original forest. Be careful where the trail runs beside the water; the agitated Green River washed out some of the bank during the floods of August 1991. After 20 to 30 minutes you'll reach the falls, where the viewpoints are fenced for added security. An interpretive sign explains the falls' geological evolution.

All of this precaution will only increase your appreciation once you've reached the bottom of the falls. Though they are almost as high as Brandywine Falls, the feeling here is quite different. Whereas the waters of Brandywine plummet straight down to a catch pool and then run off into Daisy Lake, here the Green River boils over the falls, swirls around boulders and rushes past before dropping again and disappearing with a roar into the forest. When the river's action is excited by higher-than-average run-off, pieces of driftwood shoot from the top of the falls as if from a cannon.

Aside from the drama of the falls, the park also provides a good spot for picnicking and overnight camping. A park map, several tables, and benches with a view of the Green River are located beside the visitor parking lot at the start of the falls trail. There are 88 well-spaced sites, several of them designed as doubles for visitors who are travelling in a group. (To locate the doubles, check the park map.)

When you first enter the park you will be met with a decision as to which way to turn. If you bear right past the day-use area, you will be on Green River Road. All of the sites on the right-hand side of this road have views of the river. The sound of the current creates a cocoon of privacy around each site. Surrounded by tall Douglas fir trees, these popular spots fill up quickly. During summer months this is a favourite campground with visitors to the Whistler-Pemberton region. From May to September there is a charge for overnight visitors. Each site comes with a log table and a firepit fitted with a cooking grill. Dry wood is available from a log dump behind a yellow gate across from site 57 in the middle of the campground. There's a blue water pump across from site 31 at the intersection of Maple and Green River roads.

A short trail runs down to Coudre Point, where the river widens. This is a good place for fishing and exploring the river on foot in daytime and for stargazing at night. The trail begins near the intersection of Green River Road and Dogwood Lane. Look for it between sites 14 and 46.

A much longer trail begins next to site 86 at the intersection of Green River Road and Fir Lane. Known as the Moose trail, it runs 1.9 mi. (3 km) north from the park to One-Mile Lake (where moose graze in a meadow on the south side of Signal Hill in springtime). You can easily walk to the lake and back in an hour. Interpretive signs posted beside the trail at

The Green River churns through a stone puzzle at Nairn Falls.

intervals point out interesting botanical features such as a stand of white birch or a rough-fruited fairy bell bush. This trail is fun to cycle, especially as it twists through the forest on the side of Signal Hill. There are some particularly large trees just where the trail nears the lake. You can practise the art of cutting your handlebars quickly back and forth as you snake past their trunks.

ONE-MILE LAKE   The municipality of Pemberton maintains a small day-use park beside One-Mile Lake, 1 mi. (1.6 km) north of Nairn Falls. Road access is from Highway 99, which runs along the west side of the lake. There are four picnic tables beside a large stone fireplace. A pit toilet is set back in the woods. A small beach with a floating dock invites visitors to take a plunge in the warm waters. After a camping trip in the upper Lillooet region, where the glacier-fed creeks are too cold for comfort, One-Mile Lake is a good place to wash off the dust. From the dock you can look north over the broad Pemberton Valley to the tops of the Cayoosh Range rising in the distance.

A gentle trail circles most of the lake with a boardwalk across the marshy north end where a small stream drains north into nearby Pemberton Creek. Another dock is located halfway along the lake's east side. Beside it is a small rock bench, a good place to rest with a pair of binoculars. There's plenty of waterfowl activity on the lake during spring and fall migration. According to Molly Ronayne, whose family settled in the valley several generations ago, One-Mile Creek used to drain into the lake from the mountainside above; now it's channelled into nearby Pemberton Creek. As a consequence, the water in One-Mile Lake is not as cold as it was, which has resulted in an explosion of underwater growth. By midsummer much of the lake is covered with lily pads. When you're in Pemberton, just to the north, look up to the ridge on the west—the white blur you see is a waterfall on One-Mile Creek.

23 | PEMBERTON AND AREA

Until Highway 99 linked Pemberton with Whistler and Squamish in the early 1970s, valley residents had lived in a state of semi-isolation, their only access to the rest of the province the railroad built in 1915. Now, as well as the highway to the south, there are two roads to Lillooet in the north: the Duffey Lake Road and the Hurley Road.

Because of Pemberton's remoteness, the families in the area are a proud, independent group who have made do without much outside help, relying on each other for assistance when times were hard. Many of the pioneers and their descendants, who still tend the family farms, view the provincial government's attention to the upstart Resort Municipality of Whistler with a mix of cynicism and envy. Everything that the residents of Pemberton achieved by way of government assistance and services came about after years of exhaustive petitioning of the provincial government. When you visit Pemberton, what you see is a self-made community, united by neighbourly ties based on a wealth of history and experience on the land.

Because most residents live and work on the land, downtown Pemberton is small compared to Squamish or Whistler. As you drive into town the most imposing structure is the Pemberton Hotel, next to the railway depot. This building has seen a lifetime of arrivals and departures. Since it was built 75 years ago it has been enlarged and spruced up considerably, especially since Vancouver's world's fair, Expo 86. Visitors who first came for the fair have returned in subsequent years to explore Pemberton and beyond. This small town no longer exists in isolation; with the paving of the Duffey Lake Road it is not even the end of the highway but now one of a number of towns, such as Lillooet and Lytton, that share the increased tourist traffic along the "Coast Mountain Circle Route" corridor.

Pemberton (pop. 2100) has several festivals throughout the year, and none draws more enthusiastic participation than Canada Week at the

151

Step into Pemberton's pioneer past at this authentically restored homestead, part of the Pemberton Museum.

end of June. Everyone comes in from the farm now that fields have been planted; if it's been a warm spring, the first crop of hay may even have been cut by now. Marching bands gather in the centre of town, vintage automobiles and horse-drawn carriages roll side by side, bicycles and ponies bedecked with ribbons carry excited youngsters while sports teams stand resplendent in fresh uniforms waiting for the games to begin. This is an especially colourful time to visit Pemberton. (See Cougar Mountain chapter for map of this area.)

PEMBERTON PIONEER MUSEUM Behind the hotel at the corner of Aster and Prospect streets is one of the town's prime attractions, the pioneer museum. Housed in a two-storey log cabin built originally by Will Miller, the museum is fronted by a garden of herbs, hollyhocks, and geraniums and sheltered beneath the widespread arms of a tall cedar. An old dugout canoe crafted by native carver Nicholas Joe stands next to the front porch. Parked beside it is a vintage democrat, a horse-drawn wagon used by the Oblate fathers from the early 1900s to 1955 to travel between Port Douglas and 29-Mile House on the Lillooet River.

Inside, the cabin has been lovingly restored and furnished with antiques donated by pioneer Pemberton families. It's easy to imagine living here, under the peaked roof. The museum is open to visitors during summer months, Wednesday to Sunday. At other times of the year you can peer in the windows to see the old rattan rocker next to the old pump organ in the living room, or into the kitchen with its oilcloth-covered table and hand-pumped running water.

Several more cabins and a wealth of ancient farm and logging equipment have been set up behind the museum, along with the cast-iron drive shaft from the sternwheeler Melanie that once brought travellers up Lillooet Lake from 29-Mile House to old Port Pemberton. A metal rooster surmounts the weathervane atop Sam Jim's old cabin; next door is the Barney house, built in the 1920s, once the cozy home of a family of six. If you stopped to visit Jacquie's Place on the road between Whistler and Pemberton, you will recognize its twin in John Andrew's squat, moss-chinked trapper's cabin, next to the old privy that rounds out the museum's collection. To complete the picture there is a picnic table where you can sit enjoying the view of massive Mount Currie while contemplating the fact that, no matter how humble, to the Pemberton pioneers such cabins were their castles.

PEMBERTON BACK ROADS   If you've come with a bicycle, Pemberton and its environs offer an ideal outing. Most of the roads are paved and level. Although the shoulders on the country roads are not broad, traffic doesn't pass by with the same intensity as on Highway 99. You can relax as you pedal around, looking at the homesteads and exploring some of the back roads. There are also several stables in the area, among them Adventures on Horseback (894-6155), that offer the chance to tour the valley in the saddle. If you'd rather stay behind the wheel of your car no one will mind if you poke along doing some sightseeing, as long as you leave other vehicles room to pass; otherwise, leave your car in the large parking lot in front of the hotel. From here you can choose from several different directions.

Portage Road links Pemberton with Mount Currie, 5 mi. (8 km) east. It runs in an almost straight line with farmland on either side. Just before the Lillooet River Bridge, take the well-marked Airport Road on the right. This leads south into the delta of islands created by the convergence of the Lillooet and Green rivers. The airport and golf course are located on one that is periodically inundated by floodwater. Just prior to the bridge to the airport, a rough road runs a short distance south to the Green River. A logging bridge leads across the river to a new road. When this road isn't being used by heavy equipment, you can ride or ski down along it to the west side of Lillooet Lake, 5 mi. (8 km) away. An ancient Lil'wat pictograph was recently discovered painted on a rockface near Ure Creek. For the native people who travelled this area for millennia and left little more than the footprint of their moccasins, the pictograph has great historical significance.

This road has been the scene of confrontation between native Indians

Wide-open fields are a rarity in mountain country, except in the Pemberton Valley.

seeking a settlement of their land claims and loggers desperate for work as the supply of usable timber in the Squamish Forest District dwindles. After the flooding in 1991 relations between farmers and the loggers have also soured. With almost half their seed potato crop lost and recovery forecast to take two to three years, farmers blame excessive logging in the upper Lillooet River Valley for much of the extra silt and debris washed down into the river. Drinking water in the valley must now be boiled before consumption.

To get more of a feel for "Spud Valley," head north out of town along the Pemberton Valley Road, which links Pemberton with Pemberton Meadows. This road runs up the valley for 16 mi. (26 km). As it leaves town the road rounds a corner to the right of the Esso station. Go along Prospect Street for a short distance to the intersection of Camus Street. There's a small clearing with a picnic table here, a good spot to stop to reorganize or check a map if you've biked up from Whistler or nearby Nairn Falls park. Just around the corner, Prospect Street turns into the Pemberton Valley Road.

A small ridge blocks the view here, but as you round the corner past Camus Street the valley spreads out, with the peaks of the Pacific Ranges far distant to the north. Hidden to the west is the broad Pemberton Icefield, an uninterrupted series of glaciers running from the head-waters of the Squamish River to the Upper Harrison Headwaters (as the Lillooet River system is sometimes called.) Huts maintained by the Alpine Club of Canada dot a route through the icefields over which wilderness adventurers cross-country ski in winter.

A mile north of the town centre along the valley road you pass the secondary school. This brings you to an historic T-intersection with the

Pemberton Farm Road, which originally linked Pemberton and Mount Currie. John Currie, the first European to settle in the valley, built his cabin at this intersection. The Pattenaude house on the northwest corner was originally a store and post office. It has been remodelled since it ceased operation in the 1930s. This is also the site of Agerton, where the railway station was originally intended to be located. Several decades before the Pacific Great Eastern railway line was constructed from Squamish to Quesnel in 1915, a group calling themselves the Howe Sound, Pemberton Valley & Northern Railway subdivided an area around the Pattenaude house and dubbed it Agerton. Their plans for a town and railway never materialized, but the name stuck for years afterwards.

The Pemberton Farm Road leads south from the intersection towards Portage Road, but no longer connects with it. Along the way you pass many beautiful homes, old and new, most with features characteristic in the valley: tall peaked roofs to shed heavy snow, and as many windows as possible to let in views of Mount Currie. In winter when light levels are low the windows also help stave off cabin fever.

The road dead-ends shortly after the pavement yields to gravel. If you're driving you'll have to turn around here. If you're on foot or cycling you can bear to the right of the farm gate at the end of the road. A log footbridge lies across a small stream. It connects with a neighbourhood of new homes where Portage Road crosses the railway tracks, across from the Pemberton Hotel. (Two picnic tables are situated here, perhaps for the benefit of hitchhikers waiting for a ride. There is no municipal transportation in Pemberton-Mount Currie, so those on foot must rely on the helpful nature that is a hallmark of country life.)

Resuming the journey north of the Agerton intersection, the Pemberton Valley Road wends its way gently past cleared acreage. You'll see the occasional horse or Charolais bull, but almost all the fields are given over to the cultivation of seed potatoes for export to growers in the western United States. The names on many of the mailboxes you pass along the road are those of settlers who arrived generations ago: Ronayne, Hartzell, Ryan, Miller, Garling. Many of these family names grace mountains and waterways throughout the valley. One example is Miller Creek, 3 mi. (5 km) north of Pemberton. A bridge crosses here, and again over the Ryan River where it joins the broad Lillooet River, 1.5 mi. (2.5 km) north of Miller Creek.

There are few places along the river where the public can walk or ride. Most of the dike trails that look so attractive for recreational purposes run through private property and are gated. Ask permission of the owners before travelling over them. You don't want to risk a showdown with a Charolais. (In farming country, remember to leave gates as you find them; the farmer may have closed the gate to keep livestock in, or have left it open to allow animals access to water in another pasture.)

You have now reached the heart of the valley. North of Ryan River you pass through the area called Pemberton Meadows for the next 11 mi. (18 km). Over the past decade, rural Pemberton has grown in popularity as a place to live. Pioneer families are witnessing more new arrivals than at any time since the settlement of the valley. In recent years Outward Bound, the survival-training organization, moved its headquarters to the meadows, 6.5 mi. (10.5 km) north of the Ryan River Bridge and next to the Ronayne farm. Mount Ronayne rises above on your right while imposing Mount Samson lies straight ahead to the northwest. Much of the land over which you are now travelling was reclaimed following the completion of the 15-mi. (24-km) dike system begun in 1946. The meadows stretch north to where the valley narrows and farm cultivation ends.

At the intersection 4.3 mi. (7 km) past Outward Bound, the Lillooet River Road turns to the right and heads towards the north side of the river and beyond into the Lillooet headwaters. If you do not make this turn but instead continue along the south side of the Lillooet River, you can drive on for another 12 mi. (20 km). Though there are picnic spots above the river in places, access is limited. You will eventually come to a point where the road is washed out. This was once the only road in the north end of the valley but is now very little travelled except by residents and wildlife.

24 | LILLOOET HEADWATERS

Visiting the Lillooet headwaters is like returning to the days before the dike system straightened out the Pemberton Valley section of the Lillooet River. In the headwaters north of Pemberton Meadows the river braids itself across the narrow valley floor. When it's at full flow, it leaves very little ground uncovered on either side. As seasons change and levels in the river drop, wide sandbars stand revealed, making it possible to walk well out towards the middle in many places.

Until 1975 only one road, running along the valley's south side to the foot of Spidery Peak, provided access into the headwaters. With the awarding of logging contracts around Mount Meager came the construction of the Lillooet River Forest Road. Maintaining this road has proved to be no small feat as the river has repeatedly washed out vulnerable sections. Still, the road reopens after every deluge and commercial activity resumes.

From a recreational standpoint, the Lillooet headwaters offer visitors the chance to see magnificent icefields, experience the hottest thermal springs in the province, visit the site of the most recently active volcano in southwestern B.C., and view flora and fauna ranging from rare botanicals to grizzly bears. Summer is a popular time to travel through the headwaters, while cross-country skiers and snowmobilers will find that they have the region to themselves during winter months.

The road into the headwaters begins where the Lillooet River Forestry Bridge crosses the Lillooet River 16 mi. (26 km) northwest of Pemberton. Watch for the sign on the Pemberton Valley Road that indicates where to turn right for both the Lillooet River and the Hurley-Bralorne roads. The bridge to both roads is 0.9 mi (1.5 km) north from here. There are several signs at this intersection, one of which reads "Lillooet 96 km." The Hurley-Bralorne Road is a summer route north to the upper Fraser Canyon.

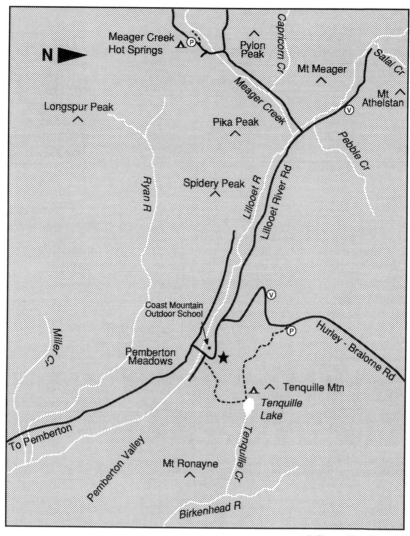

Lillooet Headwaters

As soon as you cross the wooden bridge you will see a narrow road on the right that leads back down beside the Lillooet River for 1 mi. (1.6 km). Watch for the trailhead to Tenquille Lake on your left, which heads up the mountain slope. This is the original route to the lake, first cleared in 1917. While it is not used as frequently since easier access has been provided from a new trailhead on the Hurley-Bralorne Road, it has been upgraded considerably in the past year by the Pemberton Sportsmen's Wildlife Association. Before the bridge was built Pemberton residents used to ferry themselves across the Lillooet River and hike with packhorses into the lake from here. (It's a 5-hour climb, with an elevation gain of 4818 ft. [1460 m] for those who still wish to experience it. While you do get some good views of the headwaters as you climb, the time you save by instead following the new route off the Hurley road can be better spent exploring once you've reached the lake.)

The Lillooet River road is hard-packed dirt and gravel. It's a surprisingly easy surface to cycle. Soon after the bridge, signs begin to appear, counting off the distance travelled in miles. "Mile 0" begins at the bridge (don't confuse this with Mile 0 on the historic Cariboo Trail, which begins from the town of Lillooet). There's a small group of buildings belonging to the Coast Mountain Outdoor School beside the Lillooet River a short distance past the bridge. Students visit the school (operated by the Pemberton School Board) for several days at a time to take part in an environmental awareness program. Set back across the road from the school is Heritage Village. In summer Girl Guides and other groups use the sturdy log cabins as a base for their jamborees. The centrepiece here is an old school with oversized windows that were designed to provide as much natural light as possible for learning on overcast days. On the walls inside are several large maps dating from the Dominion of Canada's early days.

The road is wide enough to accommodate large logging trucks, so be prepared to meet one coming south around one of the many bends. A pilot car usually accompanies each truck: if you pass a car with its lights flashing and the driver waving at you, it's time to pull over. Quiet time for logging traffic on the Lillooet River road is from 6 PM to 6 AM on weekdays and from Friday evening to Monday morning (careful, though—some crews work weekends, too). Also keep an eye out for deer, which come out of the forest to walk the road.

Trappers and surveyors both explored the upper Lillooet River in the early days of this century. One sign of their presence occurs between "M4" and "M5" where the road crosses Railroad Creek. This name seems strangely out of place, since the tracks are way back in Pemberton. Before the route was finally decided, surveyors considered running the line up the Pemberton Valley to this point and then climbing through Railroad Pass to reach Lillooet. Once you've driven this section you'll understand why they chose instead to route it through the gentler grade of the Pemberton (Birken) Pass.

HURLEY-BRALORNE ROAD   Over the past decade the Hurley-Bralorne Road (also called the Lillooet-Donelly Road) has been used as an alternative summer route to Lillooet. Like many similar roads in the region, this was built to carry logging equipment. It used to be that you risked losing the muffler if you attempted it in the family car. While conditions have improved somewhat, the road will still shake you up, especially if

Cycling the logging road into the Lillooet headwaters gives you a more intimate appreciation of the sights and sounds.

you drive its entire length. The views in the first 6 mi. (10 km) are worth the side trip off the Lillooet River road. Near the top of Railroad Pass you will also find the trailhead to Tenquille Lake.

The Hurley Road begins at "M5," 4.6 mi. (7.5 km) north of the bridge. It forks to the right of the Lillooet River road and is well marked. The road immediately begins to climb uphill and is marked off in kilometres. The best views of the valley below occur between "K6" and "K7." You look west towards the mountains that hold the Pemberton Icefield. The fields of the most northerly farms in the Pemberton Valley stand out below. If you position yourself here near sunset on a summer's day when water levels in the Lillooet River are low, you'll see the sandbars shade to gold as the last rays of sun stream down. The river can be seen snaking its way north to the Meager Creek Valley before tucking into the folds of its headwaters.

TENQUILLE LAKE   The trailhead to Tenquille Lake (once known as Maud Lake) is marked by a brown Forest Service sign on the right side of the Hurley road just as it crosses the bridge over Railroad Creek near the top of the pass. Park here unless you're travelling in a 4x4. If you've brought your bike you can ride in partway along an old logging road. The road meets the original trail where it climbs out of the forest. The trail begins to wind through more open fields strewn with boulders. Cycling becomes difficult beyond here. The trail climbs to a pass above the lake before descending quickly to its shore. The sides of the mountains surrounding Tenquille Lake were popular sites for miners, and there are still signs of their endeavours on the open subalpine slopes surrounding it.

In the 1940s Morgan Miller and Sandy Ross of Pemberton built a cabin beside the lake so that families from the valley could come up to visit for several days at a time (few people owned tents in those days). Built of balsam trees from the nearby slopes, the cabin is still in use with room for a dozen or more people. It's a modest structure and the beds are old, but it does provide welcome shelter, especially on wet evenings. You can warm up and dry out clothing at the small stove; the cabin may need a little cleaning when you arrive.

From here you can follow Tenquille Creek east until it meets the logging road that comes in from Gramsons near the south end of Birkenhead Lake, then loop back to Mount Currie and Pemberton. Both approaches to Tenquille Lake have been in existence since the mid-1920s. Miners preferred to use the road from Gramsons, which is twice as long but has a much gentler grade than the trail that begins from "Mile 0." Several old trails in the area surrounding Tenquille Lake are in the process of being upgraded by the Pemberton Sportsmen's Wildlife Association. An alpine trail system linking Tenquille and Owl Creek, as well as the original horse trail from Tenquille to Barber's Valley and Ogre Lake, have been constructed. The revitalizing of the trails around Tenquille make this region an exciting recreation destinations for hikers and cyclists.

UPPER LILLOOET RIVER   Past "M5" the Lillooet River road allows travellers an occasional glimpse of the river itself. For obvious reasons the road's builders tried to keep it high and away from the river to avoid washouts. If you'd like to see the river, the best places to turn off are between "M13" and "M15." Watch for side roads leading towards the river (any will do). The water in the grey-green Lillooet is always cold, fed by snow and glacier melt. As the summer progresses sandbars are revealed, side channels dry up, and it's possible to walk out onto the river. Here is a panoramic spot to fully appreciate the mountains on each side of the valley, from Mount Currie at the southern end of the valley to Mount Meager at the north.

Signs of recent forest fires are evident on the clear-cut slopes beside the road around "M20." At times when the sun catches the bare ridges above, the red rock glows as if it still held some of the heat from these blazes.

An important intersection occurs at "M25." The road to the left takes you to Meager Creek. If instead you continue on the Lillooet River road past the turnoff, you'll soon enter an area in which logging is still active. The road follows the river upstream to where Salal Creek flows into the Lillooet. Along the way the craggy volcanic spires of Mount Meager reveal themselves, including one sinister-looking crenellated black tower somewhat similar to the Black Tusk near Whistler.

A series of waterfalls cascade down the slopes of Mount Meager, draining into the Lillooet River's south side. Their roar can be heard from the road. You can explore north of "M25" in summer by bike. Once the road passes the bridge over Pebble Creek the surface deteriorates, chopped up by the heavy equipment used in logging. At the far end of the road an interesting geological formation called Pumice Bluffs is visible on the opposite side of the river. While you are exploring the Lillooet downstream in the "M13" to "M15" section, watch for pieces of this peculiar rock on sandbars or perhaps drifting by in the river. Pumice is an extremely porous rock, light enough to float. Also apparent on the slopes of Mount Meager are remnants of the lava flows that cut through the forest at the time of Meager's most recent volcanic activity. Carbon-dating of the stumps shows that they are 2500 years old.

MEAGER CREEK HOT SPRINGS   Most of the cars you'll meet as you travel north along the Lillooet River road will be heading to or from the Forest Service recreation site at the Meager Creek hot springs. In a province famous for its thermal activity, these are the hottest and most active. The water from the main spring flows at a steady 350 gal. (1325 L) per minute and has been measured in the 125°F (52°C) temperature range. These springs will test anyone's melting point—on sunny days some visitors find them to be too much. The waters in nearby Meager Creek are too swift to provide much relief except in the backwater behind some of the boulders, and even then the creek water is so cold that it is not possible to remain submerged for long. Horseflies in the area can be bothersome to the point of distraction in summer months.

Winter's chill heightens the enjoyment of the soothing hot springs beside Meager Creek. (Derrick Thompson)

On occasion they have forced me to run for the shelter of my car. Pity the poor soul who has to change a flat tire while the bugs are in season! Take along the strongest repellent you can find, but don't expect it to help much.

Even more bothersome are the carloads of yahoos who descend on the springs to party, especially on long weekends. The Forest Service has said in the past that once logging activity in the area ceases, it intends to build a berm across the road at Capricorn Creek, forcing visitors to walk, bike or ski in for the last 3 mi. (5 km). This would reduce the pollution from party-goers considerably. But the provincial government is now seeking tenders on developing the geothermal potential of the region, so it's unlikely that the road will be closed soon.

One of the best times to visit the springs is during the winter months, when the air temperature is a bracing alternative to the hot spring water (and the pesty partyers and horseflies are absent). Logging shuts down with the first snowfall and the Lillooet River Road is not as well maintained. Take chains and be prepared to snowshoe or ski in. Water

163

levels in Meager Creek are so low at this time of the year that the topography is almost unrecognizable. A series of small springs vent beside the swiftly moving creek, most too warm for comfort without the addition of some cold water. Set back off the creek is the largest source. In recent years a group known as the Friends of Meager Hot Springs has done much to improve conditions at the site. There are now two wooden tubs fed by separate springs, one of them bath temperature and the other scalding hot. Several other rock pools have been built up with cement walls to increase their depth. In the 1970s Energy, Mines and Resources did some preliminary test drilling beside the creek, sinking a pipe into one source. A small wooden sauna has been built here, with a cairn of rocks overtop the pipe to trap the heat.

To find your way to the springs, make the left turn off the Lillooet River road at "M25." Cross the Lillooet River on a rough-hewn log bridge; paddlers like to put in near here for a run on the river. Bear left at all turns on this road for the next 5 mi. (8 km). (The vast flood plain beside the road was created when Meager Creek was on the rampage in 1984.) Along the way the road crosses Capricorn Creek, which flows downhill to join Meager. Carbon-dating of stumps of trees caught in a rock slide on Capricorn Creek on the slope above the road indicate the event took place 250 years ago.

The road climbs and winds its way above Meager Creek to an important junction close to the springs. Take a left just as the road is about to enter a lumber camp equipment yard, cross the bridge that spans Meager Creek, and follow uphill to a parking area on the right above the creek. The Forest Service maintains the campsites beneath a grove of tall Douglas firs next to the parking area. A series of staircases lead down to the meadow and the springs. Camping is not permitted here. Because of the flooding that occurs regularly in Meager Creek, the botanical life in this meadow is extremely sensitive. While the small evergreens may look as if they are just beginning to grow, the fact that they have seed cones indicates they must be at least 50 years old. A variety of exotic plants grow in the marshes around the springs. Olney's bulrush is a rare sedge that has been identified in only one other area in western Canada. Its triangular stems make it easy to spot. A companion plant to the bulrush is the great northern aster, a daisy-like plant with purple petals. Yellow monkeyflower (a snapdragon lookalike) and pink fleabane (similar to a daisy) also grow near the hot water.

A vague trail behind the wooden hot tub at the north end of the meadow leads to more springs a short distance farther uphill. Thick green algae, which thrives on the carbon dioxide in the water, covers the rocks in the extremely hot pools. The source of these pools is a hot stream emanating from an outcropping of boulders. You can hear the water gurgling beneath them.

At a junction just before the logging yard, a road forks uphill to the right. It runs off along the north arm of Meager Creek for quite a distance through open fields, past Angel Falls on the slopes of Pylon Peak. Pylon Creek has a glacier buried beneath it, covered by a landslide. Next to Pylon Peak is the remnant of an old volcano called Devastator Peak. An enormous rockslide occurred on the side of the Devastator in 1975, partially blocking the flow of Meager Creek. The creek's waters backed up, creating a small lake that took several years to drain. Storms occasionally smoke up the nearby Toba or Elaho River valleys, surging in from the ocean and over the ridges of the Devastator and Pylon Peak. They make it look like Mount Meager is venting steam in preparation for the resumption of volcanic activity that geologists predict may occur within the next several centuries. Two vents spewing lethal hydrogen sulfide gas have been discovered on the north face of Mount Meager— stay well away from them. Ash from Meager's most recent eruption in 400 BC has been found as far east as the Alberta-Saskatchewan border.

There are several places along this road suitable for rough campsites should you find the crowd at the hot springs too much. Be aware that both brown and grizzly bears make this region their home.

25 | MOUNT CURRIE-D'ARCY ROAD

BOATING ◄
CAMPING ◄
CYCLING ◄
DRIVING ◄
FISHING ◄
PADDLING ◄
PICNICKING ◄
VIEWPOINTS ◄

Of all the communities in the Whistler region, Mount Currie has one of the richest histories. Long before the arrival of prospectors on the Gold Rush Trail in the 1850s, a settlement of Lil'wat people thrived at the north end of Lillooet Lake in the village of Slalock, near the present townsite of Mount Currie. According to recent archeological findings in the Fraser Valley, the Lil'wat could well have paddled their canoes in this region 10,000 years ago. But other than several rock paintings scattered throughout their extensive territory, precious few of the original inhabitants' artifacts remain to speak through the walls of time to us.

Changes undergone in the last century are but the most recent, and among the most drastic socially, experienced by a people who perfected the art of survival by maintaining the status quo. Early Europeans reported that in contrast to the hostile reception they received from the Indians of the Thompson Plateau to the east, the Lil'wat people gave them a much more gentle welcome. They were a well-dressed people whose robust good health reflected the bounty of natural wealth on which they were able to draw. That didn't mean that they weren't eager to adopt new ideas: they developed an immediate fondness for the taste of ladyfinger potatoes. Already cultivators of wild onions, their implements were perfectly suited to the new import. In the 1830s, natives brought the first seed potatoes from Fort Langley (on the Fraser River east of Vancouver and the site of B.C.'s first European settlement) home to the prairie lands around what is now Mount Currie.

Kinship with the Interior Salish (the Lil'wat are that group's most westerly members) did not shield them from attack by raiding parties, which would cross over from the Fraser Canyon on the Stein Valley Trail. One of the reasons Europeans were welcomed in Slalock was the protection they afforded residents from these hostilities. The Lil'wat also found work as guides, paddlers and packers for European travellers. Native navigational skills, developed over generations of handling cargo canoes as much as 50 ft. (15 m) in length through the Lillooet River's treacherous rapids, were very much in demand for the brief time in which travel on the Gold Rush Trail thrived.

After the gold rush played itself out, one of the newcomers decided to return and make his home in the area. John Currie married into a Lil'wat family, built a cabin in what is now Pemberton, and opened the first store and post office there. His children were among the first postal employees. In 1881 the native population of 300 or so witnessed the reduction of their traditional homeland by the provincial government from a radius of 50 miles (80 km) around Slalok to 5000 acres (2023 ha), without a treaty ever having been signed. They were simply given title to the land and told that this was where they must live. Over the next 30 years a further 1200 forested acres (486 ha) were added to their reserve (one of the largest in B.C.), mostly through acquisitions made on behalf of the Lil'wat by the Roman Catholic Church. The original settlement was relocated from the shore of Lillooet Lake to the site of the present town during this time. Locally it became known as the Rancherie, but not many people recall this name today. The official mailing address until the 1950s was Creekside; even more confusingly, this flagstop on the railway line was called Chilsampton. The name Mount Currie was chosen to end the profusion of identities.

Today there are few signs left of the old settlement along the paved road that leads east from Highway 99 to Mount Currie. But if you turn right off the main road on the north side of the Mount Currie Grocery and Mohawk gas station, drive a short distance to the Sixa-Sixa convenience store, and turn left, you'll find yourself suddenly transported back in time to the turn of the century. The street is lined with some of the older houses in the province. Built with sturdy hand-hewn beams, these rustic buildings have weathered beautifully. These are private homes, but you can visit the Sam Jim house at the Pemberton Museum to get a feeling for their snug interiors.

Halfway down the street is a treasured historic item that links Mount Currie with Whistler. The large cast-iron bell hanging in a recently constructed tower has a deep resonant sound that may be heard rolling out over the prairie on solemn occasions. Originally mounted in the Church of St. Christopher, it was lent to Whistler Mountain after a fire destroyed the church in the early 1960s. Skiers were called to lessons by its chime. In the late 1980s the bell was returned to Mount Currie and installed in this tall tower beside an open field where the church once stood. (The new church stands at the intersection of the D'Arcy and Duffey Lake roads in downtown Mount Currie.) A sheltered altar still stands here, presided over by a statue of the Virgin Mary; the Stations of the Cross are posted around the perimeter of the field.

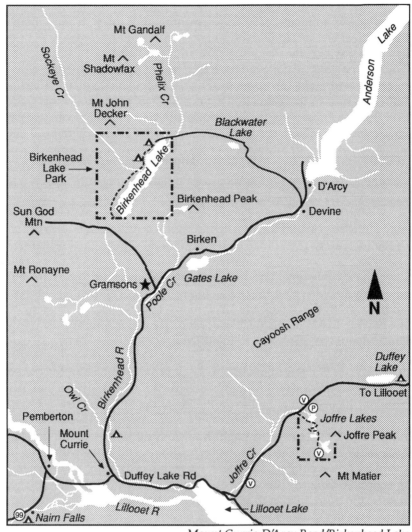

Mount Currie-D'Arcy Road/Birkenhead Lake

When weather permits, services are held outdoors. If you wish to hear the bell, visit on September 14th, the Feast of the Holy Cross, one day on which it is always rung. At that time of the year sweet peas are in full bloom in a garden across the street. Perhaps it's the influence of the clear mountain air, but these flowers have an unrivalled perfume when compared with city blossoms. (For more information on outdoor services call 894-6380. Information on other aspects of Mount Currie can be obtained by calling the town's administrative office, 894-6394.)

The historic St. Christopher's bell now rings on solemn occasions, but it was once lent to Whistler to summon skiers to lessons.

D'ARCY-ANDERSON LAKE ROAD   The 25-mi. (40-km) road linking Mount Currie with D'Arcy was an important section of the old Gold Rush Trail. Once travellers had made their way up the river and lake system to Mount Currie they still had to clear the Pemberton Pass before reaching the shores of Anderson Lake. Passengers rich enough to afford travel by stagecoach had to hang on for dear life as a teamster whipped his horses up the rocky road. Today this paved road is a pleasant journey by car, rail or bicycle. (Alex Stieda, the first Canadian to wear the yellow jersey in the Tour de France, enjoys taking riders from his Whistler cycle camps on this stretch of the historic trail.) Because the road climbs through a pass, some cyclists prefer to take their bikes to D'Arcy on the train, then cycle down the 48 mi. (77 km) to Whistler. (For information on transporting bicycles, call B.C. Rail in North Vancouver, 631-3500.)

Pemberton Pass at the south end of Gates Lake is 924 ft. (280 m) higher than the road's beginning in Mount Currie. This quiet, rolling stretch of road has a unique personality, perhaps because of the nature of the narrow Birkenhead River Valley through which much of it passes. The road to D'Arcy covers the same ground as was originally surveyed by Royal Engineers in 1860. The Birkenhead River Valley is so narrow that there isn't room for more than one trail. The existing road and the railroad bed have been laid over the old road.

There are few opportunities for farming except in the Gates Lake district, and even there cultivation is hindered by the effects of long, cold winters. As the frozen ground thaws it heaves up stones that must be cleared each year before plowing and seeding can commence. Since Hudson's Bay trader Alexander Anderson (after whom the big lake at D'Arcy is named) first entered the area 150 years ago, few European settlers have been able to make a permanent stand in this valley. Most of the current residents arrived only recently, with the influx of logging activity.

OWL CREEK   As you drive north of Mount Currie towards D'Arcy, the road climbs briefly after it crosses the railway tracks, then begins to level. At approximately 4 mi. (7 km) watch for a bridge over Owl Creek followed immediately by a clearing on the right where a hydro substation is located. It is marked by a brown Forest Service sign indicating the Owl Creek recreation site. Located at the confluence of Owl Creek and the Birkenhead River, there are eight charming, pleasantly spaced campsites here with picnic tables, fire rings and pit toilets. To reach the site you must cross the railway tracks, then turn either left or right when the road divides. To the right are four sheltered campsites at the mouth of Owl Creek; to the left are four more, on the banks of the Birkenhead River. The voices of both river and creek help mask other background sounds, creating a sense of privacy at each site.

A fish hatchery operated in this clearing beside the river from 1907 to 1937; it has since been relocated downstream, closer to Mount Currie. All that remains is the old orchard that once surrounded it. These trees still blossom in late May, while in September the river runs red with spawning chinook and coho salmon. (If you wish to visit the present hatchery, run by the Pemberton Sportsmen's Wildlife Association, turn right just before crossing the railway tracks in Mount Currie as you head north. Cross the Birkenhead River and bear left.)

The Owl Creek sites are popular with both fishermen and kayakers, who like to play on the smooth-flowing river. Exploring beside the railway tracks can be fun, especially as you walk south over the creek on

170

Massive Mount Currie dominates the skyline above the Owl Creek Forest Service campsite.

the sturdy ties of the bridge. One of the best views of Mount Currie occurs just past here, particularly near sunset as the last rays climb the mountainside to its rugged white crags, then fade away into the after-glow. If you camp at Owl Creek you may be awakened in the night by trains that sound as if they're in bed with you.

North of Owl Creek the D'Arcy Road runs past rock faces that were originally reshaped with black powder by early road builders. Because this part of the Gold Rush Trail is so smooth it's hard to connect it with the more difficult southern sections on the Lillooet Lake Road. Today fishermen quietly work their lines where prospectors with horses, mules and camels once grunted their way up the grade. (The use of camels wasn't very successful, as their smell was so offensive to other animals.) All along the Birkenhead River you will see the cars of fishermen who have pulled off to try their luck on the salmon, trout and char in the river. Drive slowly and watch for rough pull-outs. These occur frequently north of the narrow bridge crossing the Birkenhead. Not quite as scenic are the hydro lines bringing power from Bridge River to Vancouver, forced by the narrow valley to converge beside the Birkenhead.

The river is now on your left side until just south of Gramsons, where it begins to veer away to the northwest. Poole Creek takes over as a companion to the road and railway. The road crosses the Poole Creek bridge then passes several clearings on the left. Ab Gramson homesteaded here in the 1920s. A British First World War veteran, he emblazoned his colourful cabin, self-styled as "Number 10 Downing Street," with names of battle sites from that war.

A number of other creeks feed into the Birkenhead River from both sides of the valley. At Spetch Creek, on the right side halfway between Owl Creek and Gramsons, there is another recreation site. (The brown Forest Service sign at roadside is much smaller than that at Owl Creek— if you miss it you may have to double back.) The dirt road seems steep as it climbs immediately into the forest but is not hard to handle if you take it slowly. It circles past four well-spaced campsites with picnic tables, heavily sheltered by deciduous trees in summer, more open after the leaves fall. The bubbly white sound of the creek is enough to brighten any visit.

At Gramsons an unmarked gravel road runs left off the pavement, crosses the railway tracks next to the cabin and then heads northwest. Almost immediately a sign warns of active logging in the area. The rough road climbs to the south end of Birkenhead Lake and far beyond to the ridge on Tenquille Mountain. This is part of an arc that links with the Tenquille Lake trail and the Hurley road, bringing back-country adventurers into the north end of the Pemberton Valley. There is very limited public access to Birkenhead Lake on this route, and you cannot reach the Birkenhead park campsites by following it. (See the chapter on Birkenhead Lake for more information.)

The D'Arcy Road climbs past here to the highest point on the Gold Rush Trail, the Pemberton (sometimes called Birken) Pass. The course of Poole Creek leads off towards its headwaters on the side of Birkenhead Peak. The road bends northeast, skirting the lower slopes. Gates Lake appears, necklaced by the railway, with the small settlement of Birken (pop. 250) midway up its shoreline. With the white peak of Nequatque Mountain and the Cayoosh Range rising to the north, this lake always strikes me as the quintessential vision of the quiet life in Canada, one shared by citizens and visitors alike. Who hasn't dreamed of owning a cabin on such a postcard-perfect lake, with a small dock on which to sit on long, hot days? At this altitude and latitude these are precious days indeed. The growing season is short, and records kept over the past century show that frosts can strike in any month of the year. Yet the winters are said to be a touch milder and sunnier in Birken and D'Arcy than in the Pemberton Valley. If you've ever experienced the outflow of arctic air that slashes through the Pemberton Pass in winter months, you might be excused for thinking that such comparisons are academic.

If you're taken by the thought of staying here, there are five log cabins for rent at the Birkenhead Resort, back off the road among a tall stand of evergreens, and an equal number of drive-in campsites. You can rent boats and sailboards here in summer. If you really want to leave all the work to someone else, note that the Preston family operates a restaurant at the resort as well (contact the Birkenhead Resort at 452-3255).

Just north of Gates Lake, before the pavement reaches the Mars Crossing on the B.C. Rail line, a dirt road turns south, heading back beside the lake. Day-use access is much easier from this side. Each year on the second weekend in June, Birken hosts a rally, hill climb, truck pull and mud marathon event for 4x4 enthusiasts. The hill climb is always a favourite with spectators.

Gates Creek flows beside the road on its way north to Anderson Lake. Cleared fields are more common here, as are farmhouses, old and new. The turnoff to Birkenhead Lake Provincial Park occurs near the small settlement of Devine. D'Arcy is 3 mi. (5 km) north of here. If you want to experience the rocky conditions of the region firsthand, drive up the Haylmore Valley road, which leads through Devine to the ridge above. This road starts on the right side of the highway just north of the turnoff to Birkenhead park, leading first through farmland, then to a new neighbourhood, climbing the valley as it deteriorates to a 4x4 test drive.

D'ARCY-ANDERSON LAKE   The Nequatque Indian Reserve, home to natives of the Anderson Lake Band, occupies most of the land at Anderson Lake's south end. The village of D'Arcy (pop. 250) is partly on reserve land. As you enter D'Arcy you'll see a dirt road leading off to the left of the pavement, which crosses the railway tracks and heads north along Anderson Lake to Seton Portage. This is recommended for 4x4s only.

Drive to the end of the pavement and you come to the southern shores of Anderson Lake. Overlooking the lake here is Heritage Park, with a public boat launch, dock, beach, picnic tables, and ample parking. Free-range cattle are also a feature at D'Arcy—watch for them on the road. On the shores of the lake beside the railway tracks, Anderson Lake Resort has nine cottages for rent as well as room for 19 RV hook-ups. The resort's season is March to October, but you should call ahead to check availability (452-3232). The Anderson Lake Band also operates a large campground. There's usually room for all comers on their land around the banks of the Gates River where it enters the lake. Call the band office at 452-3303 for more information on camping and on the annual salmon festival in July.

Deep, dark Anderson Lake is 14 mi. (22 km) long. High, snow-covered ridges line each side: the Bendor Range on the west, and the Cayoosh Range on the east. A paddlewheeler named *The Lady of the Lake* once transported passengers and freight to Seton Portage at its north end. From there it was a short distance overland on road or narrow-gauge railway (complete with wooden rails and cars hauled by mules) to Seton Lake, at the top of which is Lillooet (once called Cayoosh Flats), Mile 0 on the trail to the Cariboo goldfields centred around Williams Lake. Despite its rather forbidding appearance, Anderson Lake has attracted a string of settlers along its western shoreline, especially at McGillivray Falls. One of the most relaxing ways to appreciate this route is to ride the B.C. Rail dayliner.

The total driving time from Mount Currie to D'Arcy is an easy 30 minutes—not long when you consider how much history lines the way.

26 | BIRKENHEAD LAKE PROVINCIAL PARK

BOATING ◀
CAMPING ◀
CLIMBING ◀
CYCLING ◀
FISHING ◀
HIKING ◀
PADDLING ◀
SNOWSHOEING ◀
SNOWMOBILING ◀
SWIMMING ◀
VIEWPOINTS ◀
WALKING ◀
X-C SKIING ◀

Finding Birkenhead Lake is similar to the story of Goldilocks and the three bears. In the surrounding region there are lakes that are too large or too small. But Birkenhead is just the right size for nearly everyone, suitable for boating of all kinds. The forest on the steep slopes surrounding the lake soaks up the sounds of outboard motors. At almost the same time that the development of Whistler Mountain was beginning to move into high gear, the provincial park at Birkenhead Lake was opened. For the first few years it was the preserve of locals, but once the Pemberton Highway opened in 1975, visitors from farther south also began to discover its beauty.

To reach the park you must follow the old Gold Rush Trail that runs from Mount Currie to D'Arcy. Just south of Anderson Lake, a well-marked gravel road opposite the small settlement of Devine leads up to Birkenhead Lake. Located 10.5 mi. (17 km) off the main road, the park is an easy 90-minute drive north of Whistler. (See previous chapter for map of this area.)

The road into Birkenhead is only 1½ cars wide, so drive cautiously and watch for hikers, cyclists, and the occasional RV. An average speed of 30 mph (50 kph) will have you at lakeside in 20 minutes. Along the way you pass Blackwater Lake, a small fishing spot with a designated Forest Service recreation site providing access. Just beyond here are a few barns and open fields, signs of the homesteading that has gone on in the area since the mid-19th century. The Hangover Ranch is the principal one.

In winter the road is plowed as far as Phelix Creek, almost at the entrance to the park. Cross-country skiers, snowmobilers, snowshoers and ice fishermen enjoy those cold, clear days. From May to October there's a fee for the main campsites (the wilderness sites are free), which includes use of the firewood piled at several locations throughout the

In winter, this same view of Birkenhead Lake would feature icefishing and snow-shoeing.

campground. Nights can be cool even in summer, but this is excellent campfire country. You may be content to sit around your blaze watching a million stars shine, or you might be inspired to walk over and join an informal singalong several sites away.

While the park is often full to capacity on the long weekends of Victoria Day, Canada Day, B.C. Day and Labour Day, at other times there is usually plenty of room. The Thanksgiving weekend in October, when early frosts bring out the colour in the surrounding forests, is an especially pretty time to be in the area. Signs on the main road beside the turnoff usually tell campers in advance if the park is full so that they can make alternative plans or head for wilderness campsites. (The signs aren't always up to date.)

There are 85 single and nine double campsites. (One of the advantages of the double campsites is the amount of room in which to set up tents and spread out. Friends travelling together in more than one vehicle can enjoy each other's company without having to tramp back and forth between separate sites.) The forest around the shore of Birkenhead Lake provides shelter and privacy for each site. Some are almost right on the beach; others are tucked in beside Phelix Creek, which flows into the lake. During dry seasons the road that runs through the campsites gets quite dusty and is heavily travelled by traffic to the boat launch; if space allows, choose a low-numbered site as close to Phelix Creek as possible to get away from the dust and noise. There are a dozen small overflow campsites for those who arrive after the park is full, but they are quite tightly spaced and little more than a place to park right beside the road.

If this sounds too civilized, there is also a wilderness area under some huge trees at lakeside that has been cleared for camping. Firepits and a rustic privy set back in the woods are the only civilized touches. You can chose to walk the 1.2 mi. (2 km) to the wilderness sites or to boat there. It takes 30 minutes to walk or paddle in. If you are approaching by water, the large red square nailed to a tree will show you where to land.

Around the point from the wilderness site, where Sockeye Creek tumbles down off the mountain slopes and creates a gravel bar, is some of the best rod-fishing on the lake. Kokanee, rainbow trout, and Dolly Varden char all wait to be tempted by a well-baited hook or fly.

A former logging road (at least 40 years old, according to one parks guide) runs along the lake's west side just above the trail to the wilderness sites. A gate bars access to motorized vehicles at the north end next to the boat launch. You can follow the road from the launch or take the trail that leads to it just above the wilderness campsites. The two trails meet at the small sign that indicates "Sockeye Creek 800 m." This road has been maintained as an emergency fire road by the park. Since there have been two major slides, effectively closing the road to all but walkers and bike riders, they may not be as keen to repair some of the small bridges and culverts as they have been in the past. The old road is fun on a bike or skis.

A major span crosses Sockeye Creek, 20 minutes' walk from the wilderness sites. Water flows full bore during freshet season. An open valley to the west reveals the distant headwaters feeding Sockeye Creek as it flows down to Birkenhead Lake. This is one of the few open areas around the lake. Looking up the creek from out on the water you can see a tall white peak in the distance to the west of the creek, with Mount John Decker in the foreground on the north side of the lake.

Viewpoints from the road are few, but 10 minutes' walk past the Sockeye Creek bridge watch for a clearing just off the road, where a stand of tightly spaced lodgepole pine appears. The open forest floor makes it easy to walk onto the ridge, from which you can see the lake below and across to Birkenhead Peak.

Forty minutes beyond Sockeye Creek is the biggest washout. Along the way the road climbs gently through shaded second-growth. This is a pleasant walk, especially early in the day. Although the view is sheltered, there is a lovely sense of calm as you walk. There are remnants of some impressive old-growth forest in places.

You will have to do some scrambling to make your way around the major slide area. The southern end of the lake is 20 minutes past here. A trail leads down to an open area, where you'll find a small picnic table and metal fireplace. An old log boom bobs next to the shoreline from where kids can cast in a line. As in most parts of this glacier-sculpted lake, the shoreline drops off quickly.

Melting snow from the surrounding peaks guarantees fresh water for Birkenhead Lake.

Directly across the way are a number of private cabins. A road leads to this end of the lake from a turnoff at "Number 10 Downing Street," the colourful cabin beside the B.C. Rail tracks south of Birken.

One of the pleasures of boating down the lake from the campsite is the view of the mountain range to the south that gradually reveals itself. Tenquille Ridge rises as a broad white wall of snow and ice stretching off to the west. The snow on all the peaks is quite white in spring and early summer before the melt reveals the darker ice beneath; the white looks especially pretty reflected in the lake. Looking north from the lake you see a long, tall ridge that separates Birkenhead from Anderson Lake. Allow 2 hours to canoe the 3.7-mi. (6-km) length of the lake. The best landing spots are on the northern half; rocky cliffs dominate other parts.

The creeks that feed the lake originate in the towering Coast Mountains that rise on all sides. Most of the creeks will have dried up by the time summer officially arrives. Their dry beds create beaches for relaxing in the sun. The best swimming is at the wide sandy beach that has been developed beside the main campsite.

The scree tumbling down off the mountain slopes in long chutes not only forms creekbeds but also allows easy access for climbers who would like to head up for a view of the lake. The views from all sides are quite lovely in this park. There is a good mix of evergreen and deciduous trees around the lake, and in autumn the forest blazes with colour.

27 | LILLOOET LAKE ROAD

BOATING ◄
CAMPING ◄
CYCLING ◄
DRIVING ◄
FISHING ◄
HOT SPRINGS ◄
PADDLING ◄
PICNICKING ◄
SWIMMING ◄
VIEWPOINTS ◄
WALKING ◄

Lillooet Lake is fed at its north end by three major rivers: the Green, the Birkenhead, and the upper Lillooet. The rivers enter the lake within a short distance of each other. The accumulation of silt at the confluence of these three major sources accounts for this being the fastest-growing delta in North America. It is estimated that in the past century over a mile (1.6 km) of waterfront has been filled in at the north end of Lillooet Lake. This is clearly evident in the land around the Mount Currie rodeo grounds, which is largely composed of sand. The buildup has been accelerated since the late 1940s by the installation of flood-control dikes in Pemberton Meadows. The silt that once fertilized those fields at flood times is now channelled downstream into the lake.

The first road skirting Lillooet Lake was built in 1858. The one that now runs along its east side is a recent arrival, accompanying the string of hydro towers that were put into service in the 1960s. Travellers today face few of the challenges experienced by the gold rush crew who passed this way; however, there are no services along this road, so be certain that you are carrying enough fuel to last the journey. One thing that hasn't changed is the beauty of Lillooet Lake. Depending on the time of day and weather conditions, the colour of the lake varies from a pale jade green to jet black.

To reach the Lillooet Lake Road, travel 9 mi. (15 km) east along the Duffey Lake Road from Mount Currie to the lakehead. A bridge spans the Birkenhead River where it enters the lake. Just beyond it, where the Duffey Lake Road begins to climb the mountainside, watch for Lillooet Lake Road turning off to the right. It's easy to spot—there's a bright orange gate at its side.

Within the first mile (0.6 km) the Lillooet Lake Road crosses over Joffre Creek, which tumbles down the last part of its run from the icefields high above. As you drive south you will notice yellow distance markers along the entire road. Also at roadside are a host of wildflowers: white daisies, pink wild roses, saffron lilies, blue lupines, and a profusion of other species and shades.

Just before the "5 km" marker is a small native graveyard on the sloping hillside between the lake and the road. There are five women buried here; the most recent grave dates from 1902. The eldest, Chief Mary Joseph, who died in 1872, may have been one of the women who brought the first potatoes to the Pemberton Valley after a trip to Fort Langley in the 1830s. The Lil'wat people had cultivated the wild onion, once prolific in the Pemberton Valley, for centuries before the arrival of Europeans, and their pointed digging implements were equally suited to potatoes.

The road gently climbs and falls beside the lake. While it is wide enough for cars going in either direction, care should be taken at several blind corners, especially as there may be cyclists on the road. Count on averaging 30 mph (50 kph) as you drive this gravel road.

LILLOOET LAKE CAMPSITES   The first of several Forest Service campgrounds along the west side of Lillooet Lake is Strawberry Point at "6 km." One of the best beaches on the lake is located here. Although the water in this big lake rarely gets warm enough for long swims, a beach where you can toast up is inviting enough. Unlike at other campsites in this area, you must park and walk into Strawberry Point. There is usually plenty of large driftwood washed up on the beach, providing shelter from the wind that often blows on the lake.

You can launch a boat onto Lillooet Lake at Twin One Creek, at the "10 km" point. A rough logging road across from the campsite leads up the north side of Twin One Creek, providing views of the north end of the lake. Between Twin One and Twin Two creeks is the Lillooet Lake Lodge with five small cabins and 10 campsites for rent. For information call 875-1160 in Vancouver.

There are even better views from above the Lizzie Bay campsite at "15 km." The sites here and at nearby Driftwood Bay (at "16 km") offer forest shelter; some sites also have their own small beaches.

LIZZIE LAKE   A logging road halfway between the Lizzie and Driftwood campsites runs up the south side of Lizzie Creek to Lizzie Lake, 7.4 mi. (12 km) east. If you take the first left turn on this road, where a sign points right to Lizzie Lake, it leads quickly up through a series of switchbacks above the lake. Along here are several good viewpoints where you can see the south and north ends of Lillooet Lake, the narrows between the large and small lakes, as well as the heights of Mount Neal and Mount James Turner (named for a climber and an Anglican minister, respectively) on the west side of the lake. The tops of Anemone Peak

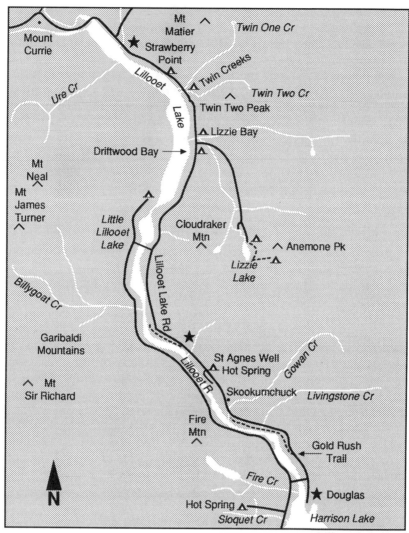

Lillooet Lake Road

and Cloudraker Mountain rise above to the east and the south. The road continues climbing up the side of the Meadow Dome, as this mountain is called, for quite a distance; the best views are in the first 2 mi. (3 km). You will notice several pull-offs that could serve as rough campsites should you have trouble finding space at lakeside.

For the first 6-mi. (10-km) of the Lizzie Lake road you shouldn't have to worry about clearance on the underside of your vehicle. For the last 1.5 mi. (2.5 km) where the road deteriorates you may want to park and walk. Active logging continues in this area and there are several new roads leading to the cutting grounds. It's not hard to tell which road leads to Lizzie Lake—it's the one road the grader clears regularly. Watch for a divide near the 6 mi. (10 km) point, with one fork continuing straight ahead and uphill while the other heads to the right. This is a good place to park. The road to the right leads to a view of the waterfall on Lizzie Creek. The road straight ahead leads uphill to Lizzie Lake. It will take you 30 minutes on foot to reach the lake from here.

There is a small privy at the trailhead. From here a rough trail leads beside the lake. At the outset there are several small clearings suitable for single tents. These little clearings also offer shelter for picnickers from the wind that often blows down from the high snowbound ridges above the lake. A strong windstorm several years ago resulted in the large blow-downs that litter the forest floor; the trail beside the lake can be an obstacle course because of them. Depending on the amount of snowmelt during late spring and early summer, it may be possible to hike up into the nearby alpine by July. The best time for visiting is midsummer through early fall. There are a number of small lakes and mountain ridges to explore in the open alpine region above the eastern end of Lizzie Lake.

The lake trail leads up through a pretty gorge aptly named the Gates of Shangri-La. At trail end is a small, popular, public cabin for overnight visitors. There often isn't room for everyone to sleep inside in summer, so plan accordingly. The trail is taped to this point. Allow 90 minutes to make the hike from the lake to the cabin.

Looking back down the wide valley to where you began the drive, you can see that this is a natural entrance into the mountains on the east side of Lillooet Lake, an approach that eventually leads into the upper Stein Valley, linking Mount Currie with Lytton, an eight-day trek. This was once the traditional trading route between the peoples of the coast and their neighbours on the Fraser River. It was also the way the Lil'wat's enemies from the Thompson Plateau would enter the Pemberton Valley on occasional raiding parties.

Even if you prefer to walk beside Lizzie Lake without exploring the mountains above, enjoy the silence of the old-growth forest and taste the waters of the lake, which are as soft as the long strands of pale green moss trailing from the branches above.

Driftwood Bay is the last of the series of Forest Service campsites on Lillooet Lake. South of here the lake narrows, then widens once again and becomes Little Lillooet Lake. At "31 km" the Tenna Bridge crosses over the lake and links up with a well-maintained logging road on the west side. If you cross here and head north alongside Lillooet Lake you will find an open campsite on a point of land favoured by fishermen near the big lake's south end. This road leads south 30 mi. (50 km) to another bridge at Fire Creek which links up once again with the Lillooet Lake Road.

THE GOLD RUSH TRAIL

The early history of the Pemberton region is integrally linked with the building of the Gold Rush Trail in the 1850s, a marvellous but brief piece of B.C. history. In the waning days of the California gold rush a new strike was reported in the B.C. interior. In 1858 alone 30,000 prospectors were drawn from around the world to this sparsely populated region. The staging area for supplies was the town of Cayoosh Flats (Mile 0), now called Lillooet, 62 mi. (100 km) northeast of Pemberton. Access to the region was extremely limited, and the cost of sending freight exceedingly high: 40 cents a pound from the Okanagan. The colonial governor of the day, James Douglas, who was located in Victoria, was determined to build a route from the coast to Cayoosh Flats that would cut this cost in half. In 1857 he sent a crew of 200 Royal Engineers, supported by a group of 500 labourers with 2000 mules, packhorses, and in later years camels, to the north end of Harrison Lake to begin work on the Gold Rush Trail. The route that was chosen followed trails that had been in use for centuries by the Lil'wat people.

Beginning from the town of Douglas, the road crew picked and hewed their way nearly 30 mi. (48 km) north, to a point where supplies could then be loaded into 30-foot (9-m) hollow-log freight

GOLD RUSH HERITAGE TRAIL South of "31 km" the Lillooet Lake Road is also referred to as the Pemberton-Douglas Forest Road. This used to be the roughest part of the journey, but in recent years the worst parts have been smoothed over. Ever since the road was first put through in the 1850s, one spot in particular has bedevilled travellers. With the recent improvements the rock outcropping called "Mile 29" on the Gold Rush heritage trail no longer eats mufflers. From this point south watch for small side roads leading down to the banks of what has become the Lillooet River once more after the interruption of Little Lillooet Lake. In several places, notably near "46 km," you can pick up traces of the old trail known as the Douglas Road. It is mossy, littered with blow-downs, and surfaced with well-worn stones, but open enough to allow exploration. Also near "43 km" and "46 km" are two historic gravesites. The one at "46 km" features a large hand-carved arch. Approach all such sites with the proper respect.

ST. AGNES WELL HOT SPRING At the "50 km" point, next to the hydro tower marked "68.2," is a small but extremely hot spring. A hotel canoes piloted by members of the Lil'wat nation. From here they were paddled north by these native navigators through the Lillooet lakes to the Pemberton Valley. In time a small paddlewheel steamer, the *Melanie*, was brought up the Douglas Road in pieces, then reassembled, whereupon it took over this chore. A road was constructed from the north end of Lillooet Lake to link with Anderson and Seton lakes, a short distance south of Cayoosh. The major challenges confronting the builders were several difficult passes that had to be breached. The Douglas Pass, north of Harrison Lake, and the Birken Pass near D'Arcy were two major obstacles. To bridge the 3-mi. (5-km) gap between Anderson and Seton lakes an ingenious little railway was constructed. Running on wooden rails and with cars hauled by mules imported from the California gold hills, the narrow-gauge affair helped with the growing momentum to reach the Cariboo. Governor Douglas could proudly point to having reduced freight costs to 18 cents a pound.

For all the effort put into the Douglas Road, it only lasted a short three years at the height of its popularity. Easier routes were being opened up through the Fraser Canyon from Yale to Lytton that spared travellers delays from deep snow or portages. You can still walk sections of the Gold Rush Trail beside the Lillooet River near the native community of Skookumchuck.

and stagecoach relay station once stood here during the gold rush. The spring, named for one of Governor Douglas's daughters, is known as St. Agnes Well. The old Douglas Road passes beside the spring. You can follow it for quite a distance north of the campgrounds along the riverbank.

The side road leading down to the hot spring is quite rocky at the outset. You may wish to park at the pull-off and walk in. Many open campsites have been cleared under a tall stand of trees. The source of the hot spring, a small jet of steaming mineralized water, is close to the Lillooet Lake Road.

There are three bathing facilities: two outdoor tubs and one under an A-frame shelter. Depending on your timing, you may be the only visitor or you may find a crowd. The water in the tubs is often so hot that it limits the amount of bathing time most visitors can endure. Therefore even if you do find the site crowded, the crush usually doesn't last long. The outdoor tubs can seat eight each. The plumbing seems to be regularly improved and has been extended to run hot and cold water to the three bathing tubs.

The nearby Lillooet River is usually running too high, fast, and cold for swimming, but the riverbank is a good place to relax after bathing in the hot spring. On the opposite side of the valley steep slopes of scree rise sharply. The rocks are covered with a gold lichen. This must have inflamed the minds of the prospecters stopping to refresh themselves on their way to the gold fields. (The springs had a reputation among early prospecters as being the only free thing in the province.) This gold lichen appears in several other rock falls along the Pemberton-Douglas Forest Road.

SKOOKUMCHUCK   Just south of the springs beside Lillooet Lake Road is the small town of Skookumchuck. Make the drive, if only to see the Church of the Holy Cross with its three steeples. There are two entrances to the town, one at each end of a loop road connecting with Lillooet Lake Road.

The front doors of the church are loosely wired shut against the elements. Through a crack in the doors you can see the elaborately hand-carved interior. While the church is obviously much more than a tourist attraction, Skookumchuck residents are justifiably proud of the building. That it is still standing after nearly a century is amazing— sooner or later almost all wooden structures come to grief in a fire, as did St. Christopher's in Mount Currie, the companion to this church.

Its design is patterned on an Oblate church in France. Standing in the midst of a dozen modest frame homes, surrounded by the forest and peaks of the Garibaldi Range, this stunning piece of folk art testifies to the strength of the builders' faith. Horses were used to drag timber to the site when the church was constructed in 1905. When the horses were exhausted, the villagers would take over the task of hauling the cedar beams.

You may hesitate to enter without an invitation and will have to be satisfied with what you can see from the outside. The first time I was there a door opened at one of the homes across the road and a young man stepped outside. "Go ahead in if you want to have a look," he called out with a wave of welcome.

The interior of the church is even more grandiose than hinted at by its baroque exterior. Italian leaded-glass windows in rich shades of green, orange, blue and yellow and a rose window above the choir loft infuse the inside of the church with brightness even on a dull day. Every piece of wood has been hand-carved, from the smallest candleholder to the life-sized statues of the Holy Family, each with its own altar. Overhead a white dove of peace floats serenely.

There is a feeling of freshness to it all. The church is not a relic, but seems as alive today as when first constructed. To better appreciate the scale of the design, climb the narrow steps to the loft. This allows a view of the inside of the tall steeples that stand poised above each staircase. Raising them into position must have been quite a feat.

The white and gold interior of Holy Cross features lovely folk art detailing.

SKOOKUMCHUCK TO HARRISON LAKE   The road south of Skookum-chuck is well maintained, and you can drive the 15.5 mi. (25 km) from here to the head of Harrison Lake in 30 minutes. If you decide to stop along the way to bushwack through the undergrowth, you'll find stretches of the heritage trail on the bank of the Lillooet River south of Gowan and Livingston creeks. When you reach Little Harrison Lake you'll also come to the steep hill leading down to the water, the first challenge tackled by the builders of the Gold Rush Trail. Unfortunately, a logging company with good intentions but no historical perspective levelled the last of the old buildings at Port Douglas in 1989. You can do some interesting exploring by boat on the sheltered waters of Little Harrison Lake, especially in the narrow channel leading to the big lake.

A bridge crosses the Lillooet River 4 mi. (6 km) north of Port Douglas. It links the Lillooet Lake Road with the logging road that runs along the west side of the river. Head north on it and you will reach the Tenna Bridge at the "31 km" point of Lillooet Lake Road. Watch carefully for extra-wide logging trucks, which are often preceded by small pilot trucks warning of their approach. If you turn left along the west side of the Lillooet River you will soon reach Harrison Lake. Unless you have a sturdy 4x4 and 5 hours, do not attempt the drive to Harrison Hot Springs at the lake's south end. The road is all but washed out in several places.

SLOQUET HOT SPRINGS   Soon after you cross the bridge over the Lillooet River 11.8 mi. (19 km) south of Skookumchuck, you will come to the intersection of the main north-south logging road and a logging road that heads west towards Fire Lake. Turn south on the main road.

Almost immediately it crosses Fire Creek. The next creek you come to is Sloquet, 1.5 mi. (2.5 km) south of the main junction. Instead of crossing it, take the rough road leading off to the right. It follows the north side of Sloquet Creek. The worst part of the road is at the very beginning before it smooths out, climbing gently through clearings as it does. There may be some signs of washouts on the road past the clearings. If you take it easy, you can probably make it as far as the washed-out bridge, 3.4 mi. (5.5 km) from the beginning of the Sloquet road. This bridge once spanned the creek that feeds into nearby Sloquet Creek. There is a clearing beside this small creek where you can park. If your vehicle has good clearance, independent four-wheel traction, and a winch, you might make it across when water levels are low in late summer; otherwise, ford the creek and do the last 2 mi. (3 km) on foot or by bike. The road is level until it nears the end, then it climbs steadily uphill. Watch for a rocky road descending to a meadow hidden on your left as the road crests the hill. The hot springs are downhill below this meadow. (The road continues farther west past here on mainly level ground for a good distance towards Stave Lake.)

The springs are quite hot and, at their source, surrounded by poison oak. If you carefully place some eggs in the water where the spring vents, they will be cooked by the time you've finished bathing. The beauty of the springs is that they gather in a large pool below a steaming waterfall directly beside the cold waters of Sloquet Creek. You can plunge back and forth between the two extremes to your heart's content.

When water levels in the creek are at their lowest you can explore up and down the riverbanks. Hot spring water vents from the rock wall at several places, especially downstream above clear swimming holes. The waters mingle to make bathing in them momentarily magical: your body can't tell if the water is hot or cold, only that it's the most refreshing sensation a weary traveller ever felt. And after coming this far, you wouldn't want to settle for anything less.

28 | DUFFEY LAKE ROAD- JOFFRE LAKES PROVINCIAL PARK

BOATING ◄
CAMPING ◄
CYCLING ◄
DRIVING ◄
FISHING ◄
HIKING ◄
HORSEBACK RIDING ◄
PADDLING ◄
PICNICKING ◄
VIEWPOINTS ◄

An old road runs between Mount Currie and Lillooet, a distance of 60 mi. (96 km). At least it used to be old—now that it has a smooth asphalt surface it seems suddenly new. Called the Duffey Lake Road (also spelled Duffy), it passes through North America's fastest-growing delta, climbs a high pass, then traverses Duffey Lake before entering sagebrush country on the Thompson Plateau. An ancient Indian trail preceded the road by thousands of years. At the time of the building of the Gold Rush Trail, Sapper Duffey (a private in the Royal Engineers who sometimes spelt his name without an *e*) was the first European to be guided along it. He reported that the 11% grade from Lillooet Lake to Cayoosh Pass was too intimidating for further consideration.

The Duffey Lake Road was first built as a logging road, then opened to the public in 1975. The residents of the Pemberton Valley welcomed it as a land route linking them with the Fraser Canyon. The old Gold Rush Trail favoured by prospectors in the 1850s required a journey across Anderson and Seton lakes to reach Lillooet at the north end of the canyon. Travel was impractical in winter months when the water routes froze over, which left the B.C. Rail's predecessor, the Pacific Great Eastern, their sole link to the outside world. As covered by mud and snow as it might be for much of the year, the Duffey Lake Road allowed vehicles access to Pemberton at the same time that the connection was made south to Whistler and Squamish.

At its southern terminus the road begins next to St. Christopher's Catholic Church in downtown Mount Currie, a 45-minute drive north of Whistler, then crosses a series of reserves (constituting much of Mount Currie) for the first 11 mi. (18 km). Because of the politically sensitive nature of relations between the Lil'wat (who have never signed a treaty ceding their lands to Canada) and various levels of the provincial and federal governments, this section of the road remains unpaved.

189

It's wide enough for two-way traffic as it follows beside the Birkenhead River. Watch for a unique stone house shaped like a tower on the left side of the road as you drive along, 0.6 mi. (1 km) past the church. (See Mount Currie chapter for map of this area.)

This is prairie country, though much of the landscape lies hidden behind tall poplar trees. The massive spread of the mountain after which the town is named rises above in the southern sky. Horses run free, or so it seems, though you'll rarely meet them on the road. But do keep an eye out for cyclists and hitchhikers, who rely on your courtesy to keep the dust down in summer and to help out with a ride when possible. If you're travelling this part of the Duffey Lake Road on a bike you'll enjoy yourself despite the dust. The only bother is the occasional barking dog. There are several spots beside the river to rest along the way to Lillooet Lake, an easy 30- to 45-minute pedal from Mount Currie. Just before you reach the lake you'll pass beside the rodeo grounds, then cross a narrow bridge over the Birkenhead River where it enters the lake.

It's hard to miss the rodeo fairgrounds. The bleachers and corrals stand empty except on the Victoria and Labour Day weekends; the wildest party anywhere in the Whistler region is held here dusk-to-dawn on Saturday nights, weather permitting or not. At age 15 local rider Wayne Andrew made his saddle-bronc debut in the 1975 Mount Currie rodeo. After a decade on the circuit he won the world championship in Albuquerque, New Mexico. Today he welcomes visitors to his WD Bar ranch opposite the rodeo grounds where he rents horses, leads tours and proudly introduces Leroy Brown, on whom he rode to glory. Just drive in. Phone 894-5669.

Beyond here the road begins to improve and you reach the beginning of the pavement. For a short distance you have Lillooet Lake for company. Silt and driftwood carried down by the Lillooet River are responsible for the in-filling at the head of the lake. There is a rough boat launch beside the bridge for those who would like to take some time to explore. If the current in the Birkenhead is gentle, try paddling upstream. There are ancient red-ochre pictographs on the cliff face below one of the hydro towers that straddle the mountainside. Even if you don't spot the stone paintings you'll be delighted by the quiet river, with its clear green water and company of herons, kingfishers and ducks.

One mile (1.6 km) past the Birkenhead River bridge the road divides. Stay left. The Lillooet Lake Road heads south, following the shoreline of the lake; the Duffey Lake Road begins to climb steeply past a sign reading "Lillooet 84 km" (52 mi.). The road soon crosses Joffre Creek tumbling down from high above. A series of switchbacks leads you to a pull-out from which you get an illustrated geography lesson on the valley below. Lillooet Lake, the rivers that feed it, and the open prairie around Mount Currie stand revealed. The new settlement of Xit'olacw

The Joffre Glacier looms over three turquoise lakes; sometimes boxcar-size chunks of ice plunge into the uppermost lake.

is visible on the hillside to the west. Shafts of sunlight beam down on the long ridges below the peak of Mount Currie, and Joffre Creek can be heard chattering in the canyon below.

Past here the Duffey Lake Road begins a gentler climb as it heads towards Cayoosh Pass. A number of small creeks flow down off the banks beside the road, adding to the volume in Joffre. Hidden from sight on the left, a massive field of glaciers called the Place Group covers the Cayoosh Range; on the right is the Joffre Glacier Group. These two icefields abut each other to the northwest of the Duffey Lake Road. Joffre Peak rises on the south side where the Matier and Anniversary glaciers, among others, predominate. From this side of the pass the peaks of the Cayoosh Range seem less imposing than those of the Bastion Range on the west side of Lillooet Lake, but once you're through the pass their full height is revealed. At 7326 ft. (2220 m) Duffey Peak is the tallest in the Cayoosh Range, but it is all but invisible from roadside.

JOFFRE LAKES PROVINCIAL PARK   Three small lakes fed by Joffre Creek lie cradled at the top of Cayoosh Pass, 15.5 mi. (25 km) north of Mount Currie. The largest of the trio is easily reached in a few minutes' walk from the parking lot. The upper two lakes are a strenuous 7.4-mi. (12-km) hike away (a trek not recommended for children under the age of 10). Close-up views of the surrounding glaciers are your reward for making the effort. Icefields around Squamish and Whistler may appear to be more accessible to local climbers, but the ones above the Joffre Lakes are actually easier to reach. The Vancouver Alpine Club opened a trail to them many years ago. As travel to the lakes became more popular the area was given status as a Forest Service recreation site and then designated a provincial park in 1988.

As you ascend the Duffey Lake Road watch for a large parking lot on the right, 7.4 mi. (12 km) past the viewpoint pull-out. There is a map of the trail system as well as a toilet and four picnic tables here, a good place to do some warm-up stretches and finalize your approach. Put on your sturdiest footwear.

Just past the tables a sign points to the beginning of the trail. Where it divides soon after, take the right fork. (The left fork leads a short distance to the shoreline of the largest lake, a good place to launch a small boat. The lake was stocked a decade ago, and according to Maggie Paquet, author of *Parks of British Columbia and the Yukon*, the fingerlings are just now beginning to reach pan-size.)

The right fork winds through the forest, muddy at the outset. A rough campsite appears beside the trail, elevated slightly above the wet moss. From a clearing the lake and the glacier-covered peaks above suddenly come into view, overwhelmingly beautiful. The lake is outlined by yellow-green reeds, and its colour intensifies as the water deepens. Once across a log bridge spanning Joffre Creek, the trail rises to higher ground and the path is drier for a while. Enjoy the view and the leisurely pace here—on the lake's far side you'll come to the toughest section of the entire hike.

As it climbs through the forest, the trail now switches back to give views of the surrounding peaks mirrored in the lake's smooth surface. A large red patch of iron-rich volcanic rock shows up vividly on the face of the range to the west. Above the lake the trail reaches a short, open stretch of debris left behind by the retreating tongue of the glacier, then enters the forest once again. Musical sounds of water and wind fill this part of the woods.

After all that concentrating on moving your feet carefully over rocks and roots, the middle lake comes as a surprise, appearing all of a sudden after a 75-minute puff. The trail crosses a lively stream over some precariously propped logs, then hugs the banks of the lake. The first wide-open views of the glacier occur here.

The hike from Middle to Upper Joffre Lake is a more relaxed one, requiring 30 minutes to complete. Near the top of the trail, where the outflow of the creek occurs, is a small waterfall. If you want to see it you'll have to bushwack over to it. There is a small cave in behind the falls, full of moss and boulders. One particularly hot day I stood beneath the chill waters, looking out through a perfect rainbow. I recommend this experience if you like cold showers, but be warned that you'll need the full power of the sun to warm up afterwards. The open shoreline of the lake is just above you—follow the trail to a sheltered spot out of the wind where you can drip dry.

At the far end of Upper Joffre Lake are the glaciers you've come to see. The trail divides as it reaches the lake, winding around the rocky shoreline in both directions. Stay to the left and you will find some good picnic spots near the outflow of Joffre Creek. Stay right for a winding journey to the far end of the lake, 30 minutes farther along. A large rock cairn marks the end of the trail and the beginning of a number of informal routes to various glaciers. From here, in 15 to 30 minutes, you could climb scree to your heart's content for an even better look. After the hike to this point I usually prefer to relax and let my eyes do the work. I like to watch as chunks of blue ice break off, exploding on the rocks below. You can admire at a distance; it's all done on such a grand scale that everyone has a good view. The adjacent icefields are more popular than ever with alpinists, who come equipped with the right gear to do some serious exploring, summer and winter. There is much terrain from which to choose, and parties of weekend climbers are as numerous as families on this trail.

The Joffre Lakes trail is as enchanting as any in the Whistler area. Take a camera to record the changes in the shape of the glaciers from one visit to the next. Times change, seasons change, even glaciers change—these huge remnants of the most recent ice age are worth regular visits just to keep tabs on their withdrawal. As they retreat they leave behind huge boulders poised at impossible angles. The time-frame and scale on which all of this activity occurs is rather humbling as you stand before it, a mere mortal. What we are privileged to witness is but a small chapter in the geological history of the world.

DUFFEY LAKE   Without leaving the Duffey Lake Road you can still experience dramatic views of the glaciers around the Joffre Lakes. The crest of the Cayoosh Pass is just above the park entrance. As you pass through it into an open valley the road levels. Drive slowly, as the views change from moment to moment. Previously concealed mountain peaks suddenly rise above the ridges, with the white snow and rutted blue ice of the glaciers spread between. Foremost among them are the Anniversary and Matier glaciers. Mount Chief Pascall, Joffre Peak, Mount Matier, and Vantage Peak present a panorama seemingly designed to use up a roll of film.

Cayoosh Creek flows along beside the road through recently logged fields. Joffre Creek Main and Van Horlick Main, two well-maintained logging roads, run off to the south of the Duffey Lake Road on the east side of Cayoosh Pass. You can drive in along Van Horlick for 8 mi. (13 km) to a campsite overlooking the Stein Valley Basin. The area is prone to slides, as evidenced by long chutes cutting down the slopes of the surrounding mountains. There were once many grizzlies here, but they are rarer now. Logging has driven much of the wildlife in the region

The 2-hour drive from Whistler to Duffey Lake is worth it for the spectacular views.

south into the rugged area at the head of Harrison Lake. (At the turn of the century the Duffey Lake region was thick with herds of mountain sheep. Cougar entered the area and within a decade had hunted down the last one.)

Duffey Lake is an easy 11-mi. (18-km) drive past the Joffre Lakes and lies at the midpoint on the road that bears its name. The town of Lillooet, the northern terminus of the Duffey Lake Road, is another 30 mi. (50 km) past here. At the east end of the lake is a drive-in boat launch and a Forest Service recreation site. Among the tall trees at the site are several camping spots and sturdy picnic tables. To the south the view of Mount Chief Pascall from lakeside is captivating. You'll want to sit quietly, enjoying it as long as the insects allow. There is often a breeze blowing that will help keep them at bay, but there is a chill edge to the wind, carried like a message from the nearby glaciers.

Duffey Lake is slender and dark, ranging in colour from olive green to black, depending on the light. Its north bank rises steeply; the south side, which the road runs along, is more open but barely more accessible. An ancient Nequatque legend, told to me by Squamish pioneer Rose Tatlow, has it that Duffey Lake is home to the spirit people. When moonlight strikes the surface they rise in their canoes. The spirits are members of two vastly different communities, each with its own leader. Chief Ne-Wah and his followers inhabit the south side and ride in golden canoes, while Chief Cul-Ne-Wah's people are from the dark side of the lake and ride in jet-black dugouts. According to the legend, after much fasting and prayer a warrior visits Chief Ne-Wah in the spirit world below the waters of Duffey Lake, where he learns to see with inner vision, in something similar to the meditation techniques of Eastern religions. As the story unfolds, it warns that not all have the strength to persist and reach the golden country—some instead succumb through laziness to the dark side. When the warrior wishes to return to the world above the waters of Duffey Lake, Chief Ne-Wah presents him with a crystal shaped like an eye that will allow him to see through all things as if they were thin air. It's heartening to imagine that those who visit the lake might come away with the same clarity of vision.

INDEX